Canada Immigration

Success Guide

A Quick Do-it-yourself Canada Permanent Residence,

Job Domination, Visa, Work & Study Permit Step by Step Guide

By

Ojula Technology Innovations

Canada Immigration Success Guide

A Quick Do-it-yourself Canada Permanent Residence, Job Domination, Visa, Work & Study Permit Step by Step Guide

Copyright © Ojula Technology Innovations

ISBN: 9798402914797

Published in the United States

Limit of Liability/Disclaimer of Warranty

This book contains information obtained from authentic and highly regarded sources. Reasonable efforts have been made to publish current, reliable data and information, but the author and publisher cannot assume responsibility for the validity of all materials or the consequences of their use. Although this book is intended to offer current, accurate and clear information, immigration is a complex process. Immigration laws and regulations can change. The content of this book is not a substitute for professional advice. All information given in this book is based on the author's own research and does not constitute technical, financial or professional advice.

The author and publisher have attempted to trace the copyright holders of all material reproduced in this publication and apologize to copyright holders if permission to publish in this form has not been obtained. If any copyright material has not been acknowledged please write and let us know so we may rectify in any future reprint.

Table of Contents

Why Immigrate to Canada?

It's a very exciting opportunity coming to Canada as an immigrant. Canada is one of the top countries in the world in which you can live and work. It's one of the most popular immigration destinations in the world because it attracts immigrants world-wide. Canada has stable economy, a very high standard of living, educated population and very low crime rates. All this make Canada a preferred choice for immigrants all over the world.

Despite the Coronavirus pandemic, Canadian Immigration is still open! Canada is accepting thousands of immigrants every month. Therefore, this is a good time to apply for Canadian Immigration permanent residency or temporary visa. The federal government of Canada is looking to bring over 340,000 permanent resident newcomers to Canada this year, and 100,000 more temporary residents! This book will teach you exactly how to become one of them.

When you become a permanent resident of Canada, you can work and live anywhere in the country. You will also have access to social services and free healthcare. You will enjoy an excellent quality of life that's filled with many job opportunities and amenities.

There are more than 100 visa and immigration programs available in Canada. Some of them are based on points, and select the candidates with the highest scores for permanent residency in Canada. There are other programs that are employer-driven. This means that the main requirement is you must arrange employment in Canada. What's more, people with Canadian education and work experience qualify for even more immigration programs!

Therefore, if you're looking to apply for Canada permanent residency, study or work in Canada, this book has a ton of the information you need. It will teach you all the steps you should take and so much more!

Feel free to skip any step (chapter or section) that does not apply to you. If you need further help in your application, don't hesitate to use my support link at the bottom of this book. I will get back to you very quickly.

1. How to Check if You're Eligible for Canada Permanent Residency

This is the very first step. Before starting the process, you have to check if you're what Canada needs. This can be checked via the **Comprehensive Ranking System (CRS) Tool**: www.cic.gc.ca/english/immigrate/skilled/crs-tool.asp.

1.1. Minimum Eligibility Criteria for Federal Skilled Worker (FSW)

To qualify to apply for express entry permanent residence under the Federal Skilled Workers (FSW) program, there are minimum eligibility requirements that you need to meet.

You will need to have a CRS score of at least 67 points out of a total of 100 in the grid used to assess candidates. Do not try to calculate your CRS score before getting at least the minimum 67 points needed to be able to apply.

If you haven't done your Education Credential Assessment (ECA), and/or passed your language tests, you can try and guess your points. You can try the free Degree Equivalency Tool from WES to have an idea on your Canadian equivalency. The free Equivalency tool is not a replacement for ECA and is only there to give you an indication of what your Canadian Equivalency may be in your official ECA results.

Keep in mind that you cannot enter the Canada express entry pool without having your ECA and language results in hand.

1.1.1. CRS Scores for Education

Education	Points (Maximum: 25 points)
Doctoral (Ph.D) degree	25
Master's or professional degree	23
Two or more post-secondary credentials (one must be for a program of at least three years)	22
Post-secondary credential of at least three years	21
Post-secondary credential of two years	19
Post-secondary credential of one year	15
Secondary (high school) diploma	5

1.1.2. CRS Scores for Work Experience

Your work experience must be within the last 10 years and must be paid work. Volunteer work and internships do not count. It must belong to type/level 0, A or B using the NOC (National Occupation Classification) code:

www.canada.ca/en/immigration-refugees-citizenship/services/immigrate-canada/express-entry/eligibility/find-national-occupation-code.html (short link: https://rb.gy/hkhc9y). It must also be continuous and stretch at least over a year (30 hours per week), or an equal amount of part-time work experience (at least 15 hours per week for 2 years).

You can accumulate your work experience from two employers, as long as both jobs fall within the same NOC.

Works Experience	Points
At least 1 year	9
2 to 3 years	11
4 to 5 years	13
6 years or above	15

1.1.3. CRS Scores for Age

Age (Years)	Points
Under 18	0
18 to 35	12
36	11
37	10
38	9

39	8
40	7
41	6
42	5
43	4
44	3
45	2
46	1
47 or older	0

1.1.4. IELTS Scores & CLB Levels

There are two official languages in Canada: French and English. Therefore, if you're a skilled worker who want to immigrate to Canada, you must prove you have language proficiency in either French or English or both. To show your proficiency in English language, you are required to take language examination that is recognized by the Canada federal government.

International English Language Testing System (IELTS) is the most recommended English language test. IELTS is used to measure your proficiency if you want to work or study. A 9-band scale is used to measure your proficiency (score of 1 for a novice through 9 for an expert).

There are two main types of IETLS Test: The Academic and the General Training.

- IELTS Academic Training - This test is taken by candidates who are applying for higher education in an English-speaking country

- IELTS General Training - This test is taken by candidates who are looking to acquire work experience or going for a training program in an English-speaking country. It's mandatory if you want to immigrate to the UK, Australia, Canada, or New Zealand.

A Candidate is tested in 4 abilities: Speaking, Listening, Reading and Writing. You have a total of 2 hours and 45 minutes to take the test. You can complete Reading, Listening and Writing sections the same day, while you can complete the listening section before or after 1 week from the other tests.

To familiarize the test scores under different language tests, the IRCC (Immigration, Refugees & Citizenship Canada) has a system known as the CLB (Canadian Language Benchmark).

Here's the table you can use to translate your IELTS score to CLB levels:

CLB Level	Reading	Writing	Listening	Speaking
10	8	7.5	8.5	7.5
9	7	7	8	7
8	6.5	6.5	7.5	6.5
7	6	6	6	6
6	5	5.5	5.5	5.5

5	4	5	5	5
4	3.5	4	4.5	4

1.1.5. CRS Scores for Language Ability

You can get a maximum of 28 points here.

First Official Language Score	Speaking	Listening	Reading	Writing
CLB9 or higher	6	6	6	6
CLB8	5	5	5	5
CLB7	4	4	4	4
Below CLB7	Not eligible	Not eligible	Not eligible	Not eligible

If you take a test for the second language, you can get additional 4 points only if you're able to score at least CLB5 in each of the four language abilities.

1.1.6. CRS Scores for Adaptability

You can get a maximum of 10 points in this.

Adaptability	Points
Spouse/partner has CLB4 or higher in English or	5

16

	French	
Principal applicant studied in Canada (minimum 2 full-time years of study at the secondary or post-secondary level)		5
Spouse/partner studied in Canada (minimum 2 full-time years of study at the secondary or post-secondary level)		5
Principal applicant worked in Canada (minimum 1 year of full-time work in NOC skill type/level 0, A or B)		10
Spouse/partner worked in Canada (minimum 1 year of full-time work in NOC skill type/level 0, A or B)		5
Principal applicant has a valid job offer		5
Principal applicant or his/her spouse or common-law partner has a *relative in Canada		5

* The relative…

- must be living in Canada

- must be 18 years or older
- must be a Canadian citizen or permanent resident
- can be your parent
- can be your grandparent
- can be your child
- can be your grandchild
- can be your sibling or your spouse's sibling (child of your parent or your spouse's parent)
- can be your aunt or uncle (or your spouse's aunt or uncle (by blood or marriage))
- can be your niece or nephew or your spouse's niece or nephew (grandchild of your spouse's parent or your spouse's parent))

No other relative is acceptable. **If you need further help in your application, don't hesitate to use my support link at the bottom of this book**.

1.1.7. CRS Scores for Arranged Employment in Canada

You can get 10 points in this if you have a full-time job offer of at least 1 year from a Canadian employer. The valid job offer has to be for continuous, paid, full-time work that is not seasonal, and in an occupation listed as Skill Type 0 or Skill Level A or B of the NOC.

You can apply for a job in Canada from outside Canada by creating an account with Job Bank here: https://www.jobbank.gc.ca/home. To be eligible, you must plan to live outside the province of Quebec. If you plan on living in Quebec, see Quebec-selected skilled workers for more information.

If you need further help in your application, don't hesitate to use my support link at the bottom of this book. I will get back to you very quickly.

2. How to Find your National Occupational Classification

You need to understand what the NOC is, and which skill type or level is eligible under the Express Entry.

The National Occupational Classification (NOC) is the official resource used by all Canadian governmental bodies in relation with job/occupational information. This is a means to provide a standard structure for analysis and assessment, gathering more than 500 NOC codes. Each NOC code represents in average 60 job titles, and each NOC is organized by skill level (A, B, C or D) or skill type (0).

2.1. Main NOC Skill Type/Levels

For immigration purposes, the main job skill types or levels are:

• Skill Type 0: occupations related to management, such as factory managers, resort managers, office managers, etc.

• Skill Level A: professional occupations that usually need a university degree, such as engineers, chemists, veterinarians, pharmacists, etc.

• Skill Level B: technical occupations that usually require a college diploma or apprentice training, such as administrative assistants, firefighters, photographers, etc.

• Skill Level C: intermediate occupation that usually needs a high school diploma, such as truck drivers, travel guides, or receptionists.

• Skill Level D: labor occupation that usually only require training, such as dry cleaners, kitchen helpers, office cleaners. messengers, etc.

You have to make sure you are using the 2016 version of the NOC. It's the most up-to-date version. The 2006 and 2011 versions still exist but are not as recent as the 2016 version that is currently in use by IRCC.

2.2. NOC Requirements for Express Entry

To be eligible under the three federal programs of Express Entry, you must have previous work experience under either skill type 0, level A or B.

How to identify your correct NOC?

You can begin by looking into the NOC website and search for the NOC job code whose description would be the most comparable to your current job. You need to base your NOC code search on **job duties and not job titles**.

Remember, focus more on job duties than job titles. So, if you find your job title and the job duties you perform here isn't consistent with what NOC has, search for the job title that has job duties that are consistent with what you currently do here in your country. You can use this link:

www.canada.ca/en/immigration-refugees-citizenship/services/immigrate-canada/express-entry/eligibility/find-national-occupation-code.html.

Job duties are the most important because when submitting your proof of work experience, it has to include your job duties. IRCC will compare your job duties with those set out in the NOC job code. You should focus on the lead statement (first paragraph) and the main duties in the NOC job code.

Another option would be to use the Job Bank website here: www.jobbank.gc.ca/home. Find a job opening that matches your current job (or any previous job) and whose job duties match yours. On the job opening page, you can find the corresponding NOC code in the "Job Market Information" page.

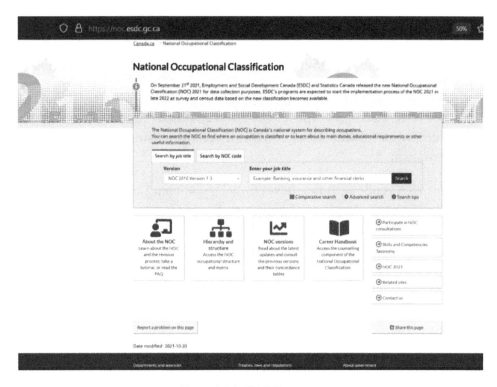

Figure 2.2.1: NOC Home page

Open the following site and scroll down to find a table containing the full list of NOC code:

www.justforcanada.com/1-finding-your-noc-national-occupational-classification.html (short link: https://rb.gy/jxisjb).

When you find your NOC, you can check your skill type or level using the table. This will let you know your NOC skill type (level 0, A, B, C or D). Find out if you're eligible to Express Entry (or to other immigration programs in future chapters).

Other Programs You Could Be Eligible to

The following are other programs that you can try, depending on the skill type/level of your NOC code:

- For NOC code skill type/level 0, A or B, you could be eligible to the **three federal programs of Express Entry**. You could also be eligible to the Atlantic High-Skilled Program of the **Atlantic Immigration Pilot program**.

- For NOC code skill type/level C, you could be eligible to the Atlantic Intermediate-Skilled Program of the **Atlantic Immigration Pilot Program**.

- For NOC code skill type/level C or D, you could be eligible to some streams of the **Provincial Nominee Programs**, such as the **Prince Edward Island PNP**, the **Northwest Territories PNP**, the **Yukon PNP**, and some others.

If you need further help in your application, don't hesitate to use my support link at the bottom of this book. I will get back to you very quickly.

3. How to Calculate your Comprehensive Ranking System Score

CRS (Comprehensive Ranking System) is a points-based system that you can use to assess and score your profile, and rank it in the Express Entry pool. You should calculate your CRS score out of a total of 1,200 points. All applicants who create their Express Entry profile are given a score out of 1,200, based on factors that play an important role in the economic success of the newcomer's once they migrate to Canada.

The following are a few factors you can use CRS to assess:

- education

- skills

- work experience

- language ability (English and/or French)

- others

3.1. Overview of the CRS

Express Entry candidates are given a score out of 1,200 based on the 4 major sections:

A. **Core / human capital factors:** these include points for Age, Education, Canadian Work Experience and Language proficiency. These are considered as key to economic success for immigrants.

B. **Spouse or common-law partner factors:** these include the accompanying spouse or common-law partner's Language proficiency, Education, and Canadian Work Experience.

C. **Skills transferability:** this section provides additional points to your profile. It's based on a combination of factors, e.g., a combination of your Education, Language proficiency, and/or Non-Canadian Work Experience.

D. **Additional points:** This section awards 600 additional points for a Provincial nomination, and other additional points for a valid job offer, etc.

The table below is a summary of the maximum points that can be awarded for each factor. Be careful to look into each factor's detailed tab to calculate your own CRS score.

Section/Factor	Maximum CRS points with spouse/partner	Maximum CRS points without spouse/partner
A & B. Core / human capital factors		
Age	100	110
Educational Level	150	150
Language Proficiency	170	160
Canadian Work Experience	80	80
Total A & B	**500**	**500**
C. Skill transferability factors		
Combination of (i) Education and (ii) Language proficiency OR Canadian work experience	50	50

Combination of (i) Non-Canadian work experience and (ii) Language proficiency OR Canadian work experience	50	50
Combination of (i) a Certificate of qualification and (ii) Language proficiency	50	50
Total C.	**100**	**100**
D. Additional points		
Provincial nomination	600	600
Valid job offer	200	200
French abilities	30	30
Sibling in Canada (citizen or permanent resident)	15	15
Total D.	**600**	**600**
Total A + B + C + D	**1200**	**1200**

3.1.1. Sections A & B. Human Capital Factors (Maximum of 500 points)

Age (Maximum points: 100 with spouse, 110 without)

Age (years)	CRS points without	CRS points with

	spouse/partner	spouse/partner
17 or younger	0	0
18	99	90
19	105	95
20 to 29	110	100
30	105	95
31	99	90
32	94	85
33	88	80
34	83	75
35	77	70
36	72	65
37	66	60
38	61	55
39	55	50

40	50	45
41	39	35
42	28	25
43	17	15
44	6	5
45 or older	0	0

Education level (Maximum points: 150)

For more information on how to get your Educational Credential Assessment (ECA) for your non-Canadian diploma, check this ECA page. Points are only awarded for the highest level of education obtained. The maximum number that can be awarded for education are 150 CRS points, either as single or with an accompanying spouse or common-law partner.

Education Level	CRS points without spouse/partner	CRS points with spouse/partner	
		Principal Applicant	Spouse/Partner
Doctoral (PhD) degree	150	140	10
Master's degree or professional degree	135	126	9
Two or more credentials, with a least one for a	128	119	9

program of three years or more			
Three-year or more post-secondary credential	120	112	8
Two-year post-secondary credential	98	91	7
One-year post-secondary credential	90	84	6
Secondary (high) school diploma	30	28	2
Less than secondary (high) school	0	0	0

Language Proficiency (Maximum points: 170 with spouse, 160 without)

You can choose your first official language after you've taken both French and English tests. The tests where you scored the highest mark is the one you should take as your first official language.

For your first official language, the following conversion table lets you know how many CRS points you can claim based on your test results. This table is per ability. For example, if you got a Canadian Level Benchmark (CLB) 7 for the four abilities (speaking, reading, listening, writing) and are single, you will get 17 x 4 = 68 points.

First Official Language Canadian Language Benchmark	CRS points without spouse/partner	CRS points with spouse/partner	

(CLB)		Principal Applicant	Spouse/Partner
CLB3 or less	0	0	0
CLB4	6	6	0
CLB5	6	6	1
CLB6	9	8	1
CLB7	17	16	3
CLB8	23	22	3
CLB9	31	29	5
CLB10 or more	34	32	5

For the second official language, the following conversion table lets you know how many CRS points you can earn per ability. There are no additional points for the second official Language, and there's no need for your spouse or common-law partner to take French and English tests. CRS points with a spouse or partner cannot exceed a total of 22 points.

Second Official Language Canadian Language Benchmark (CLB)	CRS points without spouse/partner	CRS points with spouse/partner
CLB4 or less	0	0

CLB5 or CLB6	1	1
CLB7 or CLB8	3	3
CLB9 or more	6	6

Canadian Work Experience (Maximum points: 80)

You need to find your NOC first, and then check if your job experience in that NOC is eligible here: www.justforcanada.com/4-checking-your-eligibility-to-express-entry.html.

The maximum number of points that can be awarded for Canadian work experience is 80 CRS points, either as single or with an accompanying spouse or common-law partner.

Canadian Work Experience	CRS points without spouse/partner	CRS points without spouse/partner	
		Principal Applicant	Spouse/Partner
Less than 1 year	0	0	0
1 years	40	35	5
2 years	53	46	7
3 years	64	56	8
4 years	72	63	9

5 years or more	80	70	10

3.1.2. Sections C. Skill Transferability Factors (Maximum of 100 points)

Education Level (Maximum of 50 points)

The skill transferability factors are the most important in your CRS score. You can add up to 100 points to your score, almost guaranteeing you to be drawn from the pool; however, it's not easy. For candidates in the Federal Skilled Workers program (that do not have Canadian work experience), scoring a CLB9 in all four language abilities is what could make you stand out.

For example, if you have at least CLB9 in all four abilities, and a Master's degree (which theoretically has to obtain a Bachelor's of 4 years first), you will get an additional 50 points. This is why it's extremely important to assess all your credentials with an ECA and not just your highest degree, it will not cost you more money if you do it in one take.

If you have CLB9 on all four abilities, you will not be able to add up the points for CLB7 also. It's either one or the other.

Education level + Language proficiency	Minimum CLB7 on the four language abilities	Minimum CLB9 on the four language abilities
Post-secondary education of less than 1 year	0	0
Post-secondary education of at least 1 year	13	25

At least 2 post-secondary credentials, one of which is a program at least 3 years	12	50

This can come in handy if you are eligible for the CEC (Canadian Experience Class). You could also get additional 50 points if you satisfy the conditions in the following table:

Education level + Canadian work experience	At least 1 year of Canadian work experience	At least 2 years of Canadian work experience
Post-secondary education of less than 1 year	0	0
Post-secondary education of at least 1 year	13	25
At least 2 post-secondary credentials, one of which is a program at least 3 years	25	50

You cannot get more than 50 points in this category, even if you get the 50 points from the first table, and the 50 points from the second table. You cannot get more than 100 points in this whole section C.

Foreign Work Experience (Maximum of 50 points)

The skill transferability factors are the most important in your CRS score. You can add up to 100 points to your score, almost guaranteeing you to be drawn from the pool. However, it's not easy. For candidates in the Federal Skilled Workers program, scoring a CLB9 in all four language abilities is what could make you stand out.

For example, here, if you have at least CLB9 in all four abilities, and 3 years of foreign work experience (non-Canadian), you will get additional 50 points.

If you have CLB9 on all four abilities, you won't get to add up the points for CLB7 also. It's either one or the other.

Foreign work experience + Language proficiency	Minimum CLB7 on the four language abilities	Minimum CLB9 on the four language abilities
Foreign work experience: Less than 1 year	0	0
Foreign work experience: 1 to 2 years	13	25
Foreign work experience: at least 3 years	25	50

This can come in handy if you're eligible to the Canadian Experience Class (CEC), you could also get additional 50 points if you satisfy the conditions in the following table:

Canadian + Foreign work experience	At least 1 year of Canadian work experience	At least 2 years of Canadian work experience
Foreign work experience: Less than 1 year	0	0

Foreign work experience: 1 to 2 years	13	25
Foreign work experience: at least 3 years	25	50

You can not get more than 50 points in this category, even if you get the 50 points from the first table, and the 50 points from the second table. You cannot get more than 100 points in this whole section.

Certificate of Qualification (maximum of 50 points)

This skill transferability factor concerns the candidates eligible under the Federal Skilled Trades program, that hold a valid certificate of qualification in a trade occupation issued by a competent provincial or federal authority. You can get additional 50 points if your language proficiency in the four abilities is at CLB7, and you hold a certificate of qualification.

If you have CLB7 on all four abilities, you will not get to add up the points for CLB5 also. It's either one or the other.

Certificate of qualification + Language proficiency	Minimum CLB5 on the four language abilities	Minimum CLB7 on the four language abilities
Issued a certificate of qualification	25	50

3.1.3. Sections D. Additional Factors (Maximum of 600 points)

Additional Factors

You can get up to 600 additional points. You can check the following site for more info on how to prepare your French language test:

www.justforcanada.com/3-taking-your-english-andor-french-language-tests.html (short link: https://rb.gy/nfcfya).

For provincial nominations, you need to check which provinces have an Express Entry program and that is open. You can learn all about provincial nominations here: www.justforcanada.com/provincial-nominee-programs-pnp.html.

Check this site for more information on what a valid job offer is by the standards of IRCC:

www.justforcanada.com/valid-express-entry-job-offer.html.

Additional points	Maximum 600 points
Provincial or territorial nomination acquired through an Express Entry aligned PNP stream	600
Valid job offers in NOC skill type 0 (Senior Management)	200
Valid job offers in NOC skill type/level 0, A or B	50
Completion of post-secondary program in Canada, of at least 3 years in duration	30
Completion of post-secondary program in Canada, of 1 or 2 years in duration	15

French: at least CLB7 AND English: at least CLB5 - On all four language abilities	30
French: at least CLB7 AND English: lower than CLB5or no test results - On all four language abilities	15
Sibling in Canada as Citizen or Permanent Resident	15

If during your studies in Canada you received more than 50 percent of your education via distance learning, you will not get the additional Comprehensive Ranking System (CRS) points for completion of post-secondary program in Canada.

Claiming points for Work Experience

To be able to claim any points for work experience, it must be:

- Acquired by the foreign national in Canada or outside Canada in an occupation under NOC skill type/level 0, A or B.

- Full-time (or the equivalent in part-time, at least 15hrs/week),

- Remunerated, and

- Acquired in the last 10 years.

With all of this information about the Comprehensive Ranking System (CRS), you should be able to calculate your own CRS score if you followed steps 1 to 4. You can use this tool here that will calculate your CRS score.

With all of this information about the Comprehensive Ranking System (CRS), you should be able to calculate your own CRS score if you followed steps 1 to

4. You can use the tool on this site to calculate your CRS score: www.cic.gc.ca/english/immigrate/skilled/crs-tool.asp.

If you need further help in your application, don't hesitate to use my support link at the bottom of this book. I will get back to you very quickly.

4. Getting your Educational Credential Assessment

If your diploma or degree is not from Canada, you need to get an Educational Credential Assessment (ECA). An Educational Credential Assessment (ECA) is issued to check the Canadian equivalency of a foreign degree, diploma or certificate. For example, an ECA will determine if an applicant's foreign Master's degree is of the same standard when compared to a Canadian Master's degree. If your credential is awarded in Canada by a Canadian educational body, you do need to provide an ECA.

4.1. List of IRCC-Designated Organizations

There are seven designated organizations for ECAs:

1. Comparative Education Service –University of Toronto School of Continuing Studies (CES, Date designated: April 17, 2013).

2. International Credential Assessment Service of Canada (ICASC, Date designated: April 17, 2013).

3. World Education Services (WES, Date designated: April 17, 2013).

4. International Qualifications Assessment Service (IQAS, Date designated: August 6, 2015).

5. International Credential Evaluation Service (ICES, Date designated: August 6, 2015).

6. Medical Council of Canada (professional body for Doctors) (MCC, Date designated: April 17, 2013).

7. Pharmacy Examining Board of Canada (professional body for Pharmacists) (PEBC, Date designated: January 6, 2014).

Keep in mind that ECA report must be issued on or after the date IRCC designated the organization. Most applicants will be able to get their ECA done by selecting one of the first 5 designated organizations from the above list.

If you are a specialist physician (NOC 3111) or general practitioner/family physician (NOC 3112), the Medical Council of Canada (MCC) must do the ECA for your primary medical diploma.

If you are a pharmacist (NOC 3131) and need a license to practice (for example, providing patient care in a community pharmacy, hospital pharmacy, etc.), the Pharmacy Examining Board of Canada (PEBC) must do your ECA.

ECA Validity Period

An ECA is valid for a period of 5 years from the date it is issued. To be accepted by IRCC, the ECA must not be more than five years old on the date that IRCC gets (i) your Express Entry profile, and (ii) your application for permanent residence.

Comparative Table of the 5 Designated Organizations

The price includes all the credentials you want to add. Include all your credentials, so as not to pay an additional fee and waste time if you want to assess another credential later.

	CES University of Toronto	ICAS Canada	WES	IQAS	ICES
Price (excl. taxes)	$210	$200	$220	$200	$200
Processing time	14 weeks	20 weeks	7 weeks	12 weeks	8 weeks
Canada Delivery (excl. taxes)	Standard: free Courier: 25$	Standard: N.A. Courier: 25$	Standard: $7 Courier: 25$	Standard: N.A. Courier: 15$	Standard: free Courier: 26$
International	Standard: $10	Standard: N.A	Standard: N.A.	Standard: N.A.	Standard: N.A.

Delivery (excl. taxes)	Courier: $90	Courier: $85	Courier: $85	Courier: $75	Courier: $75

The obvious choice here is WES being the quickest of them all, and not so much more expensive than the other providers. The processing time is approximate and begins once a complete application is received. Processing times can also depend on the volume of application received. We recommend using WES, and below is a guide for getting your ECA from them. I also added a few tips.

4.2. How to Apply for an ECA though WES Step by Step

Be always sure you're on the Canadian WES website, as there's a US WES as well. You can check that on the top right corner of the WES page.

Step 1: Use their free degree equivalency tool

With WES, you have an option to use the free WES degree equivalency tool at www.wes.org/ca/wes-tools before you create an account. This will give you an idea of what your ECA results may be. **This is in no way a replacement for an ECA**. The tool is simple to use and requires only the following information:

- Name

- Country of residence

- E-mail

- Country of education

- Name of Degree/Diploma

- Numbers of years of study

Then you can search for your institution. If you don't find your institution, search again but without typing anything in the box, you will get the list of all

40

institutions. Then select yours. If you still don't find your school, you can still apply through WES. Just contact WES through this link: www.wes.org/contact-us/.

Step 2: Understand the required documents (depending on your country of education)

You have to go to this page: https://applications.wes.org/required-documents. Choose your country and type of education. Depending on your answers, you will get the list of documents you need to provide. If you have a higher education diploma, the documents you will be asked to provide are:

▪ A copy (does not need to be certified) of your diploma/degree/certificate (final or provisional).

▪ An envelope with your academic transcripts for all the years you attended the institution. It does not have to be an official envelope with the name of your institution in front, but has to be either stamped or signed across the back flap by an appropriate official at your institution. You can then either ask your institution to send your sealed or signed envelope directly to WES, or send it yourself (you can send it with your other documents in one delivery).

▪ If your diploma/degree/certificate and/or your academic transcripts are not in French or English, you will need to provide in addition (do not just send the translation, send the foreign language documents too) a copy of a word-for-word French or English translation, either done by your academic institution or by a certified translation service. Translations do not need to be in the sealed envelope.

▪ If you are from some specific countries, such as Morocco, Pakistan, Nigeria, etc., you will need to have your secondary (high) school results sent to WES in a sealed envelope by the relevant body. You will need to check in the WES required-documents page.

Although it is NOT required, you can add this form: https://applications.wes.org/OnlineApp/pdf/ca/International_Transcript_Requ est.pdf. It has to be signed by you and your institution, and can help you request your documents. It has to be included in the sealed envelope and must also include the WES number you get when you register and pay your fees *(see step3).*

Step 3: Create your account and pay your fees

Go here to creates your account: www.wes.org/ca/eca/. After entering your personal information, add your credential data. You can add as many credentials as you want, it will be the same price. However, if you a credential later on, you will have to pay an additional fee. You will then have to pay the fees, either by credit card, cheque/money order, or Western Union. Once, you're done you will get your WES Reference Number.

Step 4. Gather your required documents

As discussed in step 2, the documents required depend on the country of education. After gathering them and/or have them prepared by your institution, make sure the address in the mail contains your WES Reference Number (to avoid any delays).

When sending your documents to WES, the use of express courier service is recommended. The last thing you would want is your file getting lost in transit. If this happens, you will have to restart the process. However, if you're not in a hurry, want to save some money and take the risk, you can send it by regular mail. You should check if your local postal system is trustworthy).

Step 5: Wait for the Review to be Completed

WES will review the submitted documents and communicate with you via e-mail when needed. In most cases, the evaluation will be completed in 20 business days after document submission. There will be delays if the documents submitted are incorrect or WES needs additional verification.

You can monitor the status of your application in your online WES account. You do not need to worry if your courier says the documents have been delivered but your WES status does not change, as it can take up to 3 weeks from delivery to update your status. Below are the four WES evaluation statuses:

1. Waiting for required documents.

2. Documents received – Review in Progress.

3. Waiting for verification from institution: WES may find it necessary to verify the documents you submitted with the issuing institutions. In such cases, WES will send a copy of your submitted documents to your educational institution and ask them to authenticate it.

4. Completed: you will be able to see your electronic report in your account. You will also be able to track the transit of your ECA report (hard copy) using the tracking IDs provided.

4.2.1. How to Interpret your ECA Results

A sample ECA report from WES is provided below. You need to enter the reference number at the top right of your report in your Express Entry application.

A Sample ECA Report

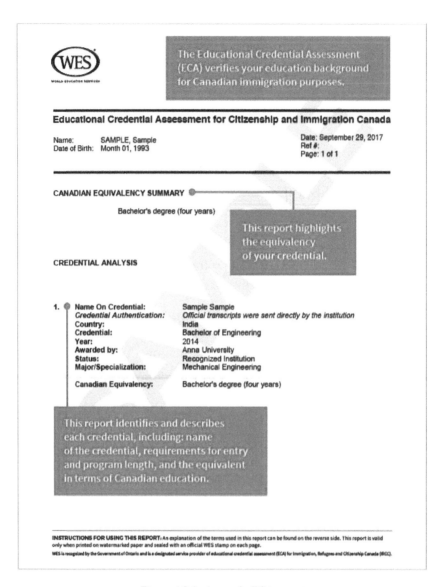

Figure 4.2.1: A sample ECA report

Depending on the results of your ECA, you can claim up to150 CRS points. If you're not sure of what your ECA report means, check out this link that contains all ECA possibilities and its CRS points equivalent:

www.canada.ca/en/immigration-refugees-citizenship/services/immigrate-canada/express-entry/documents/education-assessed/read-report.html (short link: https://rb.gy/wrvdll).

You can calculate your **overall CRS** score here:

www.justforcanada.com/5-calculating-your-comprehensive-ranking-system-crs-score.html.

If you need further help in your application, don't hesitate to use my support link at the bottom of this book. I will get back to you very quickly.

5. How to Take your English and/or French Language Tests

Language tests are one of the eligibility requirements for Express Entry. Candidates are awarded CRS points based on their English and French Language ability, but you will have to take IRCC-approved tests to earn those points (www.justforcanada.com/5-calculating-your-comprehensive-ranking-system-crs-score.html.)

Aim for at least band score of 8, 7, 7, 7 in Listening, Reading, Writing and Speaking.

5.1. IRCC-Approved Tests

There are two approved English tests and two approved French tests.

5.1.1. IRCC-Approved English Tests

1. **IELTS**: You must take the "General Training" option, not the "Academic Training". There are test locations pretty much everywhere in the world (140 countries). In the US, the fees are in ranges between $245 – $255 USD. The actual fee depends on the country. You can find a location for your test here: www.ielts.org/en-us/usa/ielts-for-test-takers. You should get your results within 14 days.

2. **CELPIP**: You must take the "General Test" option, not the "General LS Test". You can only take this test in Canada, Dubai, Chandigarh, Manila and New York. Fees vary between $265 and $340 depending on the country. You can book your test here: www.celpip.ca/take-celpip/where-do-we-test/. You should get your results within 8 business days (or 3-4 business days if you add an extra $100 to $150 fee, depending on your test location).

5.1.2. IRCC-Approved French Tests:

1. **TEF Canada**: you must take either the paper or online based (e-TEF) test. They have locations pretty much everywhere in the world and fees are around

$300, depending on the country. You can find a location for your test here: www.lefrancaisdesaffaires.fr/trouver-un-centre-agree/. You should get your results within 3 to 4 weeks.

2. **TCF Canada**: You can also take this test in various locations around the world, for fees of around $300. You can find a location for your test here: www.france-education-international.fr/centres-d-examen/carte?type-centre=tcf (short link: https://rb.gy/n0fgku). Results will be available 15 working days after the CEIP receives your session material.

There is no law that mandates you to write the IELTS exams. You could take you language assessment exam with any of the IRCC approved bodies like CELPIP, TEF Canada and TCF Canada. However, I would advise you take the IELTS over any other because of the IELTS advantages stated on this site: www.ieltsadvantage.com/.

5.1.3. Language Test Results Validity

Your test results must be less than 2 years old when you (i) complete your Express Entry profile and (ii) apply for permanent residence.

5.1.4. How to Convert your Test Results

For each test, there is a conversion table from the test mark per ability (speaking, reading, listening and writing) to the Canadian Level Benchmark (CLB). CLBs are the norm for assessing language ability by IRCC. Learn more in section 1.1.4. See conversion table below for IELTS general training:

Canadian Language Benchmark (CLB)	IELTS Test Results			

	Speaking	Listening	Reading	Writing
CLB10 and above	7.5 - 9.0	8.5 - 9.0	8.0 - 9.0	7.5 - 9.0
CLB9	7.0	8.0	7.0	7.0
CLB8	6.5	7.5	6.5	6.5
CLB7	6.0	6.0	6.0	6.0
CLB6	5.5	5.5	5.0	5.5
CLB5	5.0	5.0	4.0	5.0
CLB4	4.0	4.5	3.5	4.0

Your results, when converted to the Canadian Language Benchmark (CLB), can be used to calculate your CRS score.

Why are CRS language points so important?

Language tests are high-point earners. You will witness a significant rise in your CRS points with higher language scores. So, it is wise to practice and put in your best for the language tests. You will get more CRS language points with a better CLB. For example, for your first language and if you are single, when you improve your score from CLB7 to 8 in each ability, you will get 6 x 4 = 24 more points.

These are other additional points you could get from skill transferability factors and from French abilities:

▪ You could get 30 additional points if you have CLB7 in French and CLB5 in English (in all abilities).

▪ You could get 15 additional points if have CLB7 in French and less than CLB5 in English or no English test results at all.

▪ You could get up to additional 100 points from skill transferability factors. For more details on that, you will need to check out this CRS page: www.justforcanada.com/5-calculating-your-comprehensive-ranking-system-crs-score.html.

5.1.5. How to Prepare for your Tests

There are lots of books and study sessions available around the world that you can use to prepare for the tests. However, they may not all be free. For **free materials**, you could check the following resources:

For IELTS:

1. Sample test questions from the IELTS website:

www.ielts.org/for-test-takers/sample-test-questions.

2. When you register for an IELTS test, you will be provided with two free mock tests,

3. You can get some from this IELTS Advantages site: www.ieltsadvantage.com/.

For TEF Canada:

1. With the Français 3.0 app (www.lefrancaisdesaffaires.fr/tests-diplomes/se-preparer/francais-3-0/), you have a few free mock exam questions,

2. You can get some tutorials here:

www.lefrancaisdesaffaires.fr/tests-diplomes/se-preparer/tutoriels-tef/.

3. You can get more tutorials here:

www.france-education-international.fr/test/tcf-canada.

If you need further help in your application, don't hesitate to use my support link at the bottom of this book. I will get back to you very quickly.

6. How to Get into the Express Entry Pool

Follow the steps highlighted below to create your profile and get into in the pool of applicants. There are two main steps to enter into the pool:

(i) Use the "Come to Canada" tool to confirm eligibility and get your Personal Reference Code

(ii) Create a GCKey account and your profile to get in the pool. I will help you navigate through this process.

6.1. Using "Come to Canada" Tool

You can use the Come to Canada tool here:

www.canada.ca/en/immigration-refugees-citizenship/services/come-canada-tool-immigration-express-entry.html (short link: https://rb.gy/5nk2mx).

There is no need to provide any supporting document at this stage, note even your name. Before you start, you need only the information below:

▪ Your age.

▪ Your country of nationality,

▪ Your education qualifications: enter your highest credential as per your Educational Credential Assessment.

▪ Your relationship Status: single, married or in a common-law relationship.

▪ The number of members in your family.

▪ Your language ability: English and/or French language test results and exam dates for you, and your spouse/partner if applicable.

▪ The number of years of you work experience.

▪ If you have a valid job offer in Canada.

▪ Your destination province(s), Do not choose Quebec or you will be deemed inadmissible.

▪ The amount of money you have in your possession: www.justforcanada.com/settlement-funds.html.

You can fill in the required information in the Come to Canada tool in less than 10 minutes. Based on your answers, the tool will show whether you are eligible for Express Entry programs, and if so, will give you a Personal Reference Code (see an example in Figure 6.1.1), valid for 60 days.

6.1.1. Sample Come to Canada Eligibility Results

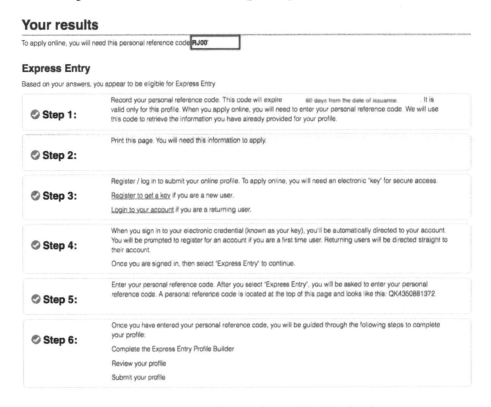

Figure 6.1.1: Sample Come to Canada Eligibility Results

6.2. Creating a GCKey Account and Express Entry Profile

You should absolutely not create an Express Entry profile if you did not take the language test(s) and gotten your ECA because you will be asked for your report numbers.

To create a GCKey account, go to this page: www.canada.ca/en/immigration-refugees-citizenship/services/application/account.html.

Then choose GCKey (the other option is for Canadian citizens or residents), and choose to sign up. You will have to choose a username, password, and 4 security questions and their answers. Make sure you remember the 4 questions and the answers you chose, as each time you connect to your account, you will be asked to answer one of these questions after entering your username and password).

Once you get inside your GCKey account, you will be able to click on an Express Entry button (see in Figure 6.2.1) to begin filling your profile.

Figure 6.2.1: The Express Entry button

When creating your profile, you'll be asked for the Personal Reference Code that you got earlier from the Come to Canada tool. Fill up the code in the relevant field, and it will automatically fill in some of the information already given in the Come to Canada tool. In order to create your Express Entry profile, you will need to enter the following information:

1. Personal Reference Code.

2. First name, middle name, last name.

3. Gender.

4. Date, country, and city of birth.

5. Marital status.

6. ID documents data.

7. Number of dependent family members.

8. Settlement funds amount.

9. Education history

10. Education Credential Assessment (ECA) date, results, and reference number.

11. Language test date, results, and reference number,

12. Work history and National Occupational Classification (NOC) codes for each work experience.

13. Passport or travel document number and expiry date.

14. Choice(s) of province.

15. Details of Provincial nomination, if applicable.

16. Details of your valid job offer, if applicable.

17. Details about your representative, if applicable.

Here's an example of a form you will fill in your Express Entry profile:

Candidate Express Entry		
Form Name	Status	Options
Personal Details	✓ Complete	Update form
Contact Details	● Not started	Start form

Figure 6.2.2: A sample Candidate Express Entry form

You will have 60 days to fill up and submit your profile. Then you will get in the pool of candidates.

If you need further help in your application, don't hesitate to use my support link at the bottom of this book. I will get back to you very quickly.

7. How to Receive an Invitation to Apply (ITA)

7.1. What's an ITA?

An Invitation to Apply (ITA) is a letter issued to a candidate drawn from the Express Entry pool, who has a CRS score above the cut-off threshold as determined in each draw. The letter is sent by Immigration Refugees and Citizenship Canada (IRCC) and received in the correspondence section of the Express Entry profile. Only after receiving the ITA that a candidate is allowed to apply for permanent residence.

When IRCC conducts a draw from the pool, candidates who meet the cut-off threshold are invited to apply for permanent residence. The receipt of an invitation to apply means the candidate is now in a position to settle in Canada with permanent resident status within a matter of months.

You can check out the latest Express Entry draw here: www.justforcanada.com/latest-express-entry-draws.html.

However, receiving an ITA does not mean you'll receive permanent residence automatically; there are crucial steps to ensure you submit the perfect application.

The number of ITA issued by IRCC to Express Entry candidates has been increased yearly since the system was put in place (2015). The upward trend will continue, as suggested by Canada's immigration plan for the period. To give you an idea:

▪ ITAs issued in 2015: 31,063.

▪ ITAs issued in 2016: 33,782.

▪ ITAs issued in 2017: 101,500.

▪ ITAs issued in 2018: 89,800.

▪ ITAs issued in 2019: 85,300.

- ITAs issued in 2020: 101,500.

What happens if you're eligible to multiple Express Entry programs?

In that case, you will be invited to apply for one program based on this order:

1. Canadian Experience Class (CEC)

2. Federal Skilled Worker (FSW) program

3. Federal Skilled Trades (FST) program

Receiving an Invitation to Apply (ITA)

IRCC issues Invitations to Apply (ITA) to candidates who are ranked highest in the pool by a process commonly called a "Draw" or "Round of Invitations". So, it is important to score high in your CRS so you get your ITA. You can find out what the latest cut-off threshold CRS score is here: www.justforcanada.com/latest-express-entry-draws.html.

If your Express Entry profile is active and your CRS score is equal or more than the cut-off score for a particular draw, then you will be issued an ITA. For some draws, not all candidates at the cut-off score received an ITA, only those who have been the longest on the pool with that score receive an ITA, depending on the total number of ITA issued.

You will receive a letter through your account. Your ITA will specify the program that you should be submitting your application for, your CRS score with a breakdown and the date by which you should submit the electronic application for permanent residence. It also provides guidance on the next steps that you can take post receiving the ITA.

An ITA is now valid for only 60 days (it was previously 90 days), and extending the deadline is not possible. It's therefore in the best interest of candidates to prepare the supporting documents beforehand, including gathering, reviewing and scanning them. The documents have to be in PDF format under 4MB. For example, some documents, such as police certificates, may need more than 60 days to be delivered by the proper authorities.

You can see the documents checklist here:

www.justforcanada.com/8-your-document-checklist-tips-and-advice.html.

What happens if you decline the ITA or let the ITA expire?

There are three scenarios that every Express Entry applicant must take note of:

▪ **If you accept the ITA:** You should submit your complete Application for Permanent Residence within 60 calendar days of ITA issue date. It's always advised to not wait till the last day as you may get negatively impacted due to unforeseen circumstances (e.g., technical issues).

▪ **If you decline the ITA:** If you decline the ITA, your profile will be moved back to the Express Entry pool and will remain active to receive future invites.

▪ **If you do not respond:** If you do not respond by "Accepting" or "Declining" the ITA then your ITA will expire and your Express Entry profile will no longer be active. You will need to create a new profile if you wish to be included in future draws.

Post Invitation to Apply

When accepting your ITA, you will be invited to fill other forms. Most of them are quite similar to the ones you already submitted for your Express Entry profile. However, you will be asked to provide more details.

You will be asked, for example, to provide your address history *and* your travel history for the past 10 years (or from your 18th birthday). This could be quite difficult for those that travel a lot. There is a maximum of 30 entries for your address or your travel history, and if you think you've travelled or changed addresses more than 30 times in the last 10 years (or from your 18th birthday), you should write Letter of Explanation (LoE) with a table retracing all that information, that you can upload with your supporting documents. You can learn more about LoE here:

www.justforcanada.com/letter-of-explanation-loe.html.

After completing your forms, a personalized document checklist page will be created and will let you upload all the necessary documents IRCC is asking for.

7.1.1. Sample ITA letter

Citizenship and Immigration Canada   Citoyenneté et Immigration Canada

Date: *******
Express Entry Profile: ******
Email: ********

Dear ********

We are writing to you about your Express Entry profile submission.

Based on the information you provided us in your Express Entry profile, we are pleased to invite you to apply for permanent residence under the ******* (

Below is the list of criteria upon which this invitation was based on:

Express Entry criteria	Your Scores
CRS – Human Capital – Age	
CRS – Human Capital – Level of Education	
CRS – Human Capital – First Official Language Proficiency	
CRS – Human Capital – Second Official Language Proficiency	
CRS – Human Capital – Canadian Work Experience	
CRS – Spouse – Level of Education	
CRS – Spouse – First Official Language Proficiency	
CRS – Spouse – Canadian Work Experience	
CRS – Skill Transferability – Education	
CRS – Skill Transferability – Foreign Work Experience	
CRS – Skill Transferability – Certificate of Qualification	
CRS – Arranged Employment	
CRS – Provincial/Territorial Nomination	
Your overall points score	

Your invitation is valid for 90 days from the date of this message.

You now have two options:
1) Decline this invitation; or
2) Apply online for permanent residence.

You must submit a complete application before *******(THE DEADLINE TO SUBMIT APPLICATION FOR PERMANENT RESIDENCE) **time if you want to apply for permanent residence.** You will not be able to submit an application based on this invitation to apply for permanent residence after the date and time listed above. We cannot give extensions.

IMM 5791 (03-2015) E GCMS   Canadä

Figure 7.1.1: A sample LoE letter

If you need further help in your application, don't hesitate to use my support link at the bottom of this book. I will get back to you very quickly.

8. Tips & Advice for your Document Checklist

In this chapter, I will give you tips and advice on how to provide all the right documents required when you receive an ITA. There's no need to upload any document during the Express Entry profile creation process. The scanned copy of your documents needs to be uploaded during your post Invitation to Apply (ITA) stage.

When should I start gathering documents?

As soon as possible! As you only have 60 days to gather all documents after receiving your ITA, you should look for the documents that might take you more than 2 months to provide. For example, some police certificates need months to be issued. You should check which police certificate you might need to apply for and check the processing times for receiving yours, and plan accordingly.

You also have to check, double-check, and then triple-check all the documents you already have, such as passports, degrees, marriage/divorce certificates etc. If you find out that there's an error or a discrepancy at the last minute, you will not be able to correct it. Take your time before getting your ITA to go through your documents multiple times so that you'll have enough time and no stress to re-issue any document that has a mistake.

When do I have to upload documents and in which format?

Your personalized document checklist is created after filling the post-ITA application forms. This checklist is dynamic and changes based on the information you have supplied in your post-ITA application form. You should provide all documents that appear in your Personalized Document Checklist.

For each of the following sections (e.g., passport, police certificates, etc.), you will have only one spot to upload your documents. If you have multiple documents to upload, you will need to merge them into *one pdf* document, that is *less than 4 MB*. You can use **SmallPDF** (https://smallpdf.com/ - free but after a few tries, you will have to wait an hour before trying again) to merge, compress or convert your documents, so you can have the right document to upload.

Applications that do not contain the following documents will likely be rejected as incomplete. To read about some common errors that previous applicants have made in their application, check this link: www.justforcanada.com/common-express-entry-refusal-reasons.html.

8.1. Documents of Identity and Marital Status

8.1.1. Passport

You have to upload a clear and readable copy of the bio page of your passport or your travel document. You should scan every page that has a marking, visa, or stamp. No need to upload blank pages. Stamps that are not in English or French must be translated. If your passport is new and contains only your biographical page, just upload that page.

Who has to upload the documents?

▪ You, the main applicant,

▪ Your spouse/partner, and

▪ Your accompanying dependent children.

8.1.2. Marriage Certificate

If you are married, documents proving this status need to be provided. The marriage has to be valid under Canadian law. If your marriage occurred in Canada, you need to provide a copy of the marriage certificate. If your marriage occurred outside Canada, a copy of the legal marriage certificate issued by the proper authorities must be provided.

Who has to upload the documents?

• You, the main applicant.

8.1.3. In a Common-law Union

If you have a common-law partner, you need to prove this status and upload the following documents:

▪ The Statutory Declaration of Common-Law Union form (IMM 5409), and

• Evidence that you and your common-law partner lived together for at least 12 continuous months, including but not limited to:

- Copy of lease agreements,

- Copy of joint bank account statements, and

- Utility invoices.

Who has to upload the documents?

• You, the main applicant.

8.1.4. Divorce Certificate

If you and/or your spouse/partner are divorced, documents proving this status need to be provided. If the divorce occurred in Canada, you need to provide either a copy of the divorce order or the certificate of divorce. If the divorce occurred outside Canada, you need to provide a copy of a legal divorce certificate issued by the proper authorities. If available, you need to also provide the copy of the legal separation agreement.

Who has to upload the documents?

• You, the main applicant, and/or

• Your spouse/partner.

8.1.5. Widowed

If you are a widow, you will need to provide a copy of a death certificate, and/or any other relevant legal document related to the death of your late spouse.

Who has to upload the documents?

• You, the main applicant.

8.1.6. Have Dependent Children

If you have dependent children, you need to upload the following documents to prove your relationship to the children:

- A birth certificate,

- Any legal document proving you are the parent, and/or

- A Letter of Explanation (in case the country of birth does not issue birth certificates).

Who has to upload the documents?

• Your dependent children, accompanying or not.

8.1.7. Having Adopted Children

If one of your dependent children is adopted, you will need to provide a copy of all relevant legal adoption documents.

Who has to upload the documents?

• Your dependent children, accompanying or not.

8.7.8. Digital Photograph

You and your family members have to provide a digital photograph meeting IRCC's specifications as stated here:

www.canada.ca/content/dam/ircc/migration/ircc/english/information/applicati ons/guides/pdf/5445eb-e.pdf (short link: https://rb.gy/munqty).

Who has to upload the documents?

• You, the main applicant,

• Your spouse/partner, accompanying or not, and

• Your dependent children, accompanying or not

8.2. Mandatory Documents

8.2.1. Medical Exam

You, your spouse/partner and your dependent children, must see a doctor on the list of panel physicians in your country. Learn more here: https://secure.cic.gc.ca/pp-md/pp- list.aspx?_ga=2.225532825.2099460414.1515531121- 1655530662.1515374155 (short link: https://rb.gy/ftqa0b).

 The panel physician will do a complete medical exam. The doctor may refer you for chest x-rays and laboratory tests. Once your exam is done, the physician will send IRCC the results. The medical exam should only be done after receiving your Invitation to Apply (ITA). Find out more on what to expect here: www.justforcanada.com/medical-exam-for-canadian-visa.html.

You must provide a copy of either

(i) the information printout sheet (for the e-Medical system), or

(ii) the Upfront Medical Report form (for the paper-based system), whichever the panel physician provides upon completion of the medical examination.

Under exceptional circumstances (at IRCC's discretion), the following may be accepted (without any guarantee):

- Proof that you scheduled the medical exam with an approved panel physician, and/or

- A Letter of Explanation (LoE) clarifying why the medical exam could not be done.

Who has to upload the documents?

• You, the main applicant,

• Your spouse/partner, accompanying or not, and

• Your dependent children, accompanying or not.

8.2.2. Police Certificate

The applicant needs to retrace his/her life from the age of 18, and calculate the number of days spent in a specific country. If the consecutive total exceeds 6 months, the applicant needs to provide a police certificate. Before getting an Invitation to Apply, the applicant should check how to get the police certificate and how long that would take. This will help smooth and relieve the stress of not getting the police certificate in time.

The IRCC website lets you know what to do to obtain the right police certificate: www.canada.ca/en/immigration-refugees-citizenship/services/application/medical-police/police-certificates/how.html (short link: https://rb.gy/lxhxfu).

Police certificates are required up front and are mandatory for each country (except Canada) where an individual has lived for a total of 6 consecutive months or more in the last 10 years. There is no need to provide police certificates for periods before the age of 18.

(i) For the current country of residence, the police certificate needs to be issued maximum six months before the application for permanent residence is submitted.

(ii) For a past country of residence (6 consecutive months), the police certificate needs to be issued after the date of departure from the country as a resident.

You should check the validity of the police certificate, if there is one. If the criteria in (i) or (ii) are respected, the police certificate may be accepted if expired. If not, you can't upload an expired police certificate.

For the police certificate of a set of countries, IRCC needs a consent form, which will allow them to ask for the police certificate directly. For example, an applicant seeking a police certificate from New Zealand must download and complete the Consent to Disclosure of Information (NZ) form available on the IRCC website. You only need to upload the consent form for this set of countries.

You need to scan (in color) the original police certificate (s). Under exceptional circumstances (at IRCC's discretion), the following may be accepted (without any guarantee):

- Proof that the police certificate has been requested immediately after receipt of the ITA, and

- A Letter of Explanation (LoE), clarifying why the police certificate could not be uploaded in time.

Who has to upload the documents?

• You, the main applicant,

• Your spouse/partner, accompanying or not, and

• Your dependent children over 18 years old, accompanying or not.

8.2.3. Settlement Funds

This is not for CEC and Applicants with Job offer.

To prove you own enough money (above the LICO (Low Income Cut-Off: www.justforcanada.com/settlement-funds.html), you have to upload a letter from at least one bank, which details all your asset accounts (cash, investments, etc.) and your debt accounts (loans, credit card debts).

- This letter has to include the letterhead and contact information of the bank, your name, account(s) numbers, opening date of the account(s), the current and average (over past 6 months) balance of the account(s).

- You need to provide proof of origin of any incoming large amounts of money that cannot be explained by your job salary. For example, a notarized gift deed. If you received large sums of money from your family within 6 months from applying, or the sale agreement of your car, land, house, etc.

For more information, check www.justforcanada.com/settlement-funds.html.

Who has to upload the documents?

• You, the main applicant.

8.3. Documents for Claiming CRS Points

8.3.1. Work Experience

If you were a salaried employee, you need to upload a reference letter from your employer, which:

- Has to include the company letterhead and contact information, your name, and the name, title and signature your superior or HR officer, and

- Has to include all occupations held during your employment within the company, with the following details: title, duties, beginning date of employment, if currently working or not in the company (end date of employment if not), number of work hours per week, and annual wages and benefits.

If you are self-employed, you need to upload evidence that you own your business, and proof of your income from clients in the form of any document explaining the service provided and payment details (if you declare your duties by yourself through an affidavit or declaration, it will not be accepted by IRCC as proof of work experience).

If you have problems coming up with an experience letter per IRCC's guidelines above, you should upload as many documents as possible from the following:

- Your pay stubs.

- Your employment contracts.

- Your job description with the company letterhead (sealed or signed by the company if possible).

- A reference letter from your supervisor (with or without the company letterhead) with as much information as possible, and most importantly your job duties, signed and legalized.

- A certificate of employment and/or salary from your employer.

- Proof that your employer refused to provide the document per IRCC guidelines.

- A Letter of Explanation (LoE) explaining why you could not provide the requested document(s).

The duties and responsibilities in your Reference Letter are very important. You can find Employment Reference Letter sample here. www.justforcanada.com/employment-reference-letter-sample-canada.html.

Your application will most likely be refused if you do not provide IRCC with this particular information. IRCC needs to compare the duties you provided with those set in the NOC page, and be confident that there is a match between the two. This is why you need to choose your NOC carefully (www.justforcanada.com/1-finding-your-noc-national-occupational-classification.html), as explained in the first step of this guide.

Who has to upload the documents?

• You, the main applicant, and/or

• Your spouse/partner.

8.3.2. Studies

To receive points for studies, you must either:

- Upload proof of having completed studies in Canada (secondary or post-secondary), or

- Upload the copy of the Educational Credential Assessment (ECA), provide its reference number in your Express Entry application, and upload proof of having completed these studies outside Canada.

Proof of completed studies in Canada or outside Canada can include copies of:

- The credentials: copy of your certificate, diploma or degree, and/or

- School transcripts showing you completed the requirements of your credential.

To obtain the additional points for studies in Canada, you must add the institution number of **Designated Learning Institution (DLI)** where you completed your highest credential: www.canada.ca/en/immigration-refugees-citizenship/services/study-canada/study-permit/prepare/designated-learning-institutions-list.html.

Who has to upload the documents?

• You, the main applicant, and/or

• Your spouse/partner.

8.3.3. Valid Job Offer

If you have a valid job offer from a Canadian employer, you must upload the letter of employment, and it must:

• Include the letterhead and contact information of the company, your name, and the name, title and signature of your future immediate superior or HR officer, and

• Include the job start date, occupation title, duties, and numbers of work hours/week, annual salary and benefits. The letter must also clarify that the job is on a continuous and full-time basis, for at least one year after issuance of the PR visa. It must also specify you are holding said job currently.

If your employer has a positive Labour Market Impact Assessment (LMIA), you need to upload the LMIA number in your Express Entry application. You do not need to upload the LMIA when submitting your application, however, it might be asked of you later by IRCC.

For more information on the validity of employment offers, go here: www.justforcanada.com/valid-express-entry-job-offer.html.

Who has to upload the documents?

• You, the main applicant.

8.3.4. Relative in Canada

This is requested if you, and/or your spouse/partner, indicate that you have a family member in Canada. Such person must be a Canadian citizen or a permanent resident. You will need proof of your family member's Canadian citizenship or permanent residence: copy of passport, birth certificate, permanent residence card, etc. (copy of both sides when applicable).

You will also need to prove that your family member is living in Canada: mortgage documents, lease, utility bills, etc. showing the Canadian address and a recent date (maximum 6 months before submission).

You have to prove as well the family member's relationship to you or your spouse/partner: official documents stating the relationship between the two family members, birth certificates, etc.

Who has to upload the documents?

• You, the main applicant, and/or

• Your spouse/partner.

8.4. Other Documents

8.4.1. Other Name

This is requested if you (or someone in your application) have used another name in the past (e.g., a maiden name). You must upload any document explaining the use of this other name (e.g., a letter of explanation, legal documents of a name change, notarized affidavit of one and same name, etc.).

Who has to upload the documents?

•You, the main applicant,

•Your spouse/partner, accompanying or not, and/or

•Your dependent children, accompanying or not.

When do I write a Letter of Explanation (LoE)?

If you feel like a document you are submitting might raise the slightest question from an immigration officer, you should add a Letter of Explanation (LoE) to your documents. For example, if it concerns your passport section, then add your LoE to the PDF file that you will upload to the passport section.

When and how to translate documents?

Translations in Canada

If any of your documents is not written in French or in English, you must also upload:

• A French or English translation, and

• An affidavit or attestation from the person who completed the translation.

- If the translation was done in by a certified translator (member of a territorial or provincial organization of translators and interpreters in Canada), they have to provide an attestation, which states that the translation is accurate and true.

- If the translation was done by an uncertified translator, they must submit an affidavit (signed in the presence of a commissioner of oaths, stating that the translation is accurate and true).

Translations outside Canada

If one of your documents is not written in French or in English, you must also upload a French or English translation by a certified translator. The translator needs to be a member of a professional translation association, evidenced by a membership number or stamp in the certified translation.

In both cases, you cannot ask one of your family members (father, mother, brother, sister, spouse, partner, grandfather, grandmother, son, daughter, uncle, aunt, nephew, niece, or first cousin) to translate your documents, it will not be accepted.

As a precaution, you should get your documents translated by a certified translator.

If you need further help in your application, don't hesitate to use my support link at the bottom of this book. I will get back to you very quickly.

9. From AOR to PPR

Once you've uploaded all requested documents, the system will take you to pages related to Declaration, Disclosure and Electronic signature. After you've indicated you agree to the Declaration, Disclosure and Electronic signature pages, you will see a table with a summary of fees that you need to pay for your e-APR (electronic Application for Permanent Residence). You can pay your fees using Visa, American Express or Mastercard debit/credit card.

9.1. The Processing Fees & Proof of Funds

There're three fees you will have to pay:

1. Processing Fee for you and your family members:

When you apply, you need to pay a processing fee for everyone who will come to Canada with you on your application. The processing fee is $550 per person, and $150 for each dependent child. IRCC won't refund the processing fee once they have begun processing your application. However, if your application isn't complete, IRCC will refund your processing fee.

2. Right of Permanent Residence Fee:

The right of permanent residence fee is $490 per person. There is no fee for dependent children. You can either pay this fee early at the same time as your Processing Fee, or when IRCC approves your application. Paying this fee early may speed up the application process. IRCC will refund this fee if you withdraw your application or if your application is refused.

3. Biometrics fee:

If you're from a country that requires your biometric data, you and your family members (except children under the age of 14) must provide biometric data. For an individual applicant, the cost is $85, and for a family applying jointly, the fee is $170.

4. Proof of Funds:

"Proof of Funds" is how you prove that you have enough money to settle in Canada. If you've got an invitation to apply, you have to give a written proof you have this money.

Why do you need Proof of Funds?

You need proof of funds to meet the minimum requirements of the

- Federal Skilled Worker Program

- Federal Skilled Trades Program

Who does not need proof of funds?

You don't need to show that you have enough money to support yourself and your family if

- You're applying under the Canadian Experience Class or

- You're authorized to work in Canada and you have a valid job offer, even if you apply under the Federal Skilled Worker Program or the Federal Skilled Trades Program.

Keep your funds up to date in your profile. The system may find that you're eligible for more than 1 program. You don't always know ahead of time which program you'll be invited under.

How much money will you need?

The amount of money you need to support your family depends on the size of your family. To calculate the size of your family you must include

- Yourself

- Your spouse or partner

- Your dependent children
  (www.cic.gc.ca/english/immigrate/sponsor/aod-tool.asp) and

- Your spouse's dependent children

Include your spouse or dependent children even if they're

- Permanent residents or Canadian citizens

- Not coming to Canada with you

This table shows the minimum amount you need to immigrate to Canada. If you have more money, you should list the full amount in your profile or application.

Number of family members	Funds required (in Canadian dollars)
1	$13,213
2	$16,449
3	$20,222
4	$24,553
5	$27,847
6	$31,407
7	$34,967

Each additional family member	$3,560

9.1.1. What's accepted as Proof of Funds

Funds must be readily available to you. For example, you can't use equity on real property as proof of settlement funds. Also, you can't borrow this money from another person. You must be able to use it to pay the costs of living for your family (even if they aren't coming with you).

If your spouse is coming with you, you can count money you have together in a joint account. You may be able to count money in an account under their name only, but you must prove you have access to the money.

The funds must be available both when you apply and when (or if) you're issued a permanent resident visa. You must prove to an immigration officer that you can legally access the money to use in Canada when you arrive. For proof, you must get official letters from any banks or financial institutions where you're keeping money.

- Letter(s) must be printed on the financial institution's letterhead.

- Include their contact information (address, telephone number and email address).

- Include your name.

- List outstanding debts such as credit card debts and loans

Include, for each current bank and investment account, the

- Account numbers

- Date each account was opened

- Current balance of each account

- Average balance for the past 6 months

Fund Requirements Update

The minimum amount you need is updated every year, and is based on 50% of the low-income cut-off totals. The changes are not much, but there's a good chance they could affect your eligibility. Therefore, ensure you search for the new numbers online (or use my support link).

9.1.2. How Much Money Should You Bring?

Find out how much it will cost you to live where you plan to settle in Canada. Go with as much money as you can get. This will ensure moving to and finding a home in Canada easier for you. Upon your arrival in Canada, you must let the border officer know if you're bringing over 10,000 Canadian Dollars into Canada. If you don't do this, you could be fined and your funds seized.

Learn more about the documents you need to cross the border here: https://www.canada.ca/en/immigration-refugees-citizenship/services/new-immigrants/prepare-life-canada/border-entry.html (short link: https://rb.gy/kojnkq)

This money includes:

1. Cash

2. Documents showing property or capital payable to you, like:

- Bonds

- Stocks

- Treasury bills

- Debentures

3. Written documents that guarantee you payment of a certain amount of money that is payable to you, like:

- Cheques

- Banker's drafts

- Traveler's cheques

- Money orders

All that funds stated above are in Canadian Dollars, not US Dollar. These funds are not to be paid to anyone. They should be within your possession. However, you would be required to show a proof you have it because they want you to be able to show you can take care of yourself when you get there.

Furthermore, no lumpsum must reflect in your account. The money there must have been gradually built over time. If you have any lump sum, you must attach a Letter of Explanation (LoE) to your bank records to show that you recently liquidated an asset into cash or you received a cash gift from a relative (must not be a loan).

There are some other fees you have to pay that can vary based on the circumstances of the individual. Police report and medical exams are not free but it depends on your location and negotiating power/skill. It would also cost you money to send your transcripts through a trackable courier express. Also, different schools charge different amounts to send transcripts on behalf of their students.

9.1.3. Receiving your Acknowledgment of Receipt (AOR)

After you've submitted your electronic Application for Permanent Residence (e-APR), you will be given an Acknowledgement of Receipt (AOR). This is the confirmation that your application for permanent residence in Canada has been received by Immigration Refugees and Citizenship Canada (IRCC) and that a file with your application number has been created. This is popularly known as *AOR date*, which marks the beginning of your six months intended processing time.

After receiving your AOR, you must report any significant change to your circumstances to IRCC, for example, a change:

- in circumstances like if you lose your job offer, a Territorial or Provincial nomination.

- in family composition, for example, if you have a newborn child, adopted a new child, a divorce or marriage occurs, etc.

- of home address or e-mail address.

- of your immigration representative.

Status updates from AOR to PPR

Generally, your application will follow the following path after receiving your AOR. This is the trend that happens with most of the applicants. It may or may not match with your application process:

• **Background check: Not Applicable (NA1)** - As soon as you submit your EE application, and receive your AOR, the "Background check" section of your application status will say "Not applicable". This status will generally not change until your medical results are reviewed and validated.

• **Review of medical results: Medicals passed (MEP)** - Approximately one month after your AOR, you should receive this message: 'You passed the medical exam'. It will typically take more time for applicants with a provincial nomination.

▪ **Background check: In Progress (IP1)** - Either the same day, one or two days after the MEP update, your "Background check" section will change to "Your application is in progress. We will send you a message when we start your background check."

▪ **Background check: Not Applicable (NA2)** – After your IP1 is finished, your "Background check" section will revert to "Not Applicable." Most of the time, IP1 only takes a few hours, and if you do not check your account during that short window, you may miss the update.

▪ **Background check: In Progress (IP2)** – The "Background check" status message will change to "We are processing your background check. We will send you a message if we need more information". After completion of the IP2 stage, the Passport Request (PPR) e-mail is sent if the applicant already paid the Right of Permanent Residence Fees upfront. PPR e-mails take 7 to 20 days after the IP2 stage.

▪ **Background Check: Not Applicable (NA3)** – This means that IP2 is finished. This "Background check" status will not be displayed in some cases, and PPR is triggered while the IP2 status is still visible.

▪ **PPR: Passport Request** - You will receive the golden e-mail directly to your e-mail account and you may not get an update in your Express Entry account. You should check your junk e-mail folder, as the e-mail does not come from IRCC but from your Visa Office (usually).

▪ **CoPR: Confirmation of Permanent Residence**. Generally, messages will be like shown in Figure 9.1.1 right after your AOR:

Figure 9.1.1: Application status updates

9.2. Frequently Used Acronyms in Visa Processing

The following are some of the acronyms frequently used in this guide and during Visa processing:

CLB - Canadian Language Benchmark.

ECA - Education Credential Assessment.

EE - Express Entry.

ROI - Round of Invitations.

ITA - Invitation to Apply.

CoPR - Confirmation of Permanent Residency

PPR - Passport Request

PR - Permanent Resident (Residency)

Keep a close eye on the e-mail you attached to the application form because you would be contacted through that email for any reason such as biometrics, more tests, etc. Most applications get processed within 6 months of the application submission dates, which is the AOR (acknowledgement of receipt) date.

Finally, note that you must arrive in Canada before your medicals or passport expires (whichever comes first).

If you need further help in your application, don't hesitate to use my support link at the bottom of this book. I will get back to you very quickly.

10. Atlantic Immigration Pilot Program (AIPP)

The government of Canada first launched AIPP in 2017. It was supposed to end on December 31, 2021 but following its success, IRCC has now made it a permanent immigration program. IRCC will release details on the program in 2022, and will resume accepting applications under the program on March 6, 2022. Candidates who are currently holding a valid endorsement letter under AIPP have to wait until that date to apply under the new program.

The Atlantic Immigration Pilot Program brought over 10,000 new permanent residents to Canada since it first opened. Among the key sectors extending job offers include health care, accommodations, food services and manufacturing.

The Atlantic Immigration Pilot is a pathway to permanent residence for skilled foreign workers and international graduates who want to work and live in one of Canada's four Atlantic Provinces. This is an employer-driven program designed to help employers in Atlantic Canada hire qualified candidates for jobs they have been unable to fill locally.

To immigrate to Atlantic Canada through the pilot,

- You must be a recent graduate of a publicly funded institution in Atlantic Canada or a skilled worker who meets the program requirements.

- You can be living abroad or already be in Canada temporarily.

- You must receive a job offer from a designated employer in Atlantic Canada to participate in the pilot.

If you receive a job offer from an employer:

- Ask for a copy of the employer's Confirmation of Designation, or

- Tell them about the Atlantic Immigration Pilot and ask them to consider becoming designated, if they aren't already.

There are 3 programs in the pilot that employers can hire you through. You may qualify for more than one program, but you can only apply through one.

For all the 3 programs, you have to show a proof that you meet the language, education and work experience requirements, and that you have enough money to support you and your family when you arrive in Canada.

The 3 programs in AIPP. They are:

• Atlantic International Graduate Program

• Atlantic High-Skilled Program

• Atlantic Intermediate-Skilled Program

10.1. Atlantic International Graduate Program

For this program, you must have schooled or lived in one of the Atlantic provinces for at least 16 months within the last 2 years. This is basically for people who currently live or school in Canada but would like to apply for PR (permanent residence).

10.2. Atlantic High-Skilled Program

Eligibility

1. Work experience

In the last 3 years, you must have worked 1,560 hours at least. This is how many hours you would have worked in 1 year if you were working 30 hours per week. This work must have been at National Occupational Classification (NOC) skill type/level 0, A, or B.

To calculate your hours:

- Count the number of hours worked in both part-time and full-time jobs.

- The hours worked must be in 1 occupation, but can be with different employers.

- You must have received payment for these hours. Unpaid work such as internships or volunteering do not count.

- Don't count the hours worked when you were self-employed.

- All working hours can be outside or inside Canada.

- The hours you worked must have been accumulated over a period of not less than 12 months.

2. Education

You must have one of the following:

- A Canadian secondary (high school) or post-secondary certificate, diploma or degree.

- A foreign degree, diploma or certificate, equal to a Canadian credential. You'll need an Educational Credential Assessment (ECA) report from a recognized organization to show your credential is valid and equal to a Canadian credential. If you already have an ECA report, it must be less than 5 years old when your permanent resident application is received.

3. Language

You must take one of the approved language tests. The test shows you can communicate in English and/or French well enough to live and work in Canada. CLB 4 and above is acceptable for this program. If you have taken an approved test, you can send those results if they:

- Are less than 2 years old

- Show you meet the level the program requires

4. Proof of Funds

You need to have sufficient money to support you and your family when you arrive in Canada. The amount you need depends on the size of your family. This includes anyone you support but is not immigrating with you.

Number of Family Members (including those you support that are not immigrating with you)	Funds Required (in CAN$)
1	$3,303
2	$4,112
3	$5,055
4	$6,138
5	$6,962
6	$7,852
7	$8,742
For each additional family member	$890

If you're already working and living in Canada with a valid work permit, you don't need to show proof of funds.

Job offer requirements

You must have a job offer that meets all of these requirements:

▪ The job offer was made using the Offer of Employment to a Foreign National [IMM5650] PDF form. Download it here: https://www.canada.ca/content/dam/ircc/migration/ircc/english/pdf/kits/forms/imm5650e.pdf (short link: https://rb.gy/oxr3da).

▪ The employer has been designated as an employer taking part in the Atlantic Immigration Pilot by the Atlantic province (New Brunswick, Newfoundland and Labrador, Nova Scotia, or Prince Edward Island) where you'll be working. They must have a Confirmation of Designation from the province.

▪ The job must be full-time, meaning you'll work at least 30 paid hours per week.

▪ The job must be non-seasonal. In general, this means you have consistent and regularly scheduled paid employment throughout the year.

▪ The job is skill type/level 0, A or B under the NOC.

▪ The employer is offering you a job that will last for at least 1 year.

You must meet employment requirements for the job you are offered. You can find these requirements in the NOC. The job doesn't need to be in the same NOC as other jobs you've had.

10.2.1 When to Submit your Application

When you and the employer have completed all the steps, you can submit your application. To save time, start filling in your permanent resident application before all of the steps are completed. Gather the documents that go with your application as soon as you can. Check out the following site to learn more and download the forms needed for the application: Application for the Atlantic High-Skilled Program: https://www.canada.ca/en/immigration-refugees-citizenship/services/application/application-forms-guides/guide-

5424-atlantic-immigration-pilot-program-atlantic-high-skilled-program.html (short link: https://rb.gy/xgxq4g).

10.3. Atlantic Intermediate-Skilled Program

Eligibility

1. Work experience

In the last 3 years, you must have worked at least 1,560 hours. This is how many hours you would have worked in 1 year if you worked 30 hours per week. Here is how to calculate your hours:

You can use your work experience to qualify for the intermediate-skilled worker program in 2 different ways.

- Count the number of hours worked in both part-time and full-time jobs.

- The hours worked must be in 1 occupation, but can be with different employers.

- You must have received payment for these hours. Unpaid work such as internships or volunteering do not count.

- Don't count the hours worked when you were self-employed.

- All working hours can be outside or inside Canada.

- The hours you worked must have been accumulated over a period of not less than 12 months.

Option 1

You have work experience at National Occupational Classification (NOC) skill level C. NOC skill level C is a type of job that usually requires a secondary (high school) education and/or job- specific training, such as:

▪ Industrial butchers

▪ Long-haul truck drivers

▪ Food and beverage servers

Option 2

You have work experience:

• As a registered nurse or registered psychiatric nurse (NOC skill level A 3012), or

• As a licensed practical nurse (NOC skill level B 3233), and

• You have one of the following job offers:

- A nurse's aide, orderly or patient services associate (NOC skill level C 3413), or

- A home support worker (NOC skill level C 4412)

2. Education

You must have one of the following:

• A Canadian secondary (high school) or post-secondary certificate, diploma or degree

• A foreign degree, diploma, or certificate equal to a Canadian credential. You need an Educational Credential Assessment (ECA) report from a recognized organization to show your credential is valid and equal to a Canadian credential. If you already have an ECA report, it must be less than 5 years old when we receive your permanent resident application.

3. Language

You must take one of the approved language tests. It will show you can communicate in English and/or French well enough to live and work in Canada. CLB 4 and above is acceptable for this program.

If you have taken one of the approved tests, you can send those results if they:

• Are less than 2 years old and

• Show you meet the level the program requires

4. Proof of Funds

You need to have enough money to support yourself and your family when you get to

Canada. The amount you need depends on the size of your family. The size of your family includes anyone you support but is not immigrating with you.

Number of Family Members (including those you support that are not immigrating with you)	Funds Required (in CAN$)
1	$3,303
2	$4,112
3	$5,055
4	$6,138
5	$6,962

6	$7,852
7	$8,742
For each additional family member	$890

If you're already working and living in Canada with a valid work permit, you don't need to show proof of funds.

Job offer requirements

You must have a job offer that meets all of these requirements:

▪ The job offer was made using the Offer of Employment to a Foreign National [IMM5650] PDF form. Download it here: https://www.canada.ca/content/dam/ircc/migration/ircc/english/pdf/kits/forms/imm5650e.pdf (short link: https://rb.gy/oxr3da).

▪ The employer has been designated as an employer taking part in the Atlantic Immigration Pilot by the Atlantic province (New Brunswick, Newfoundland and Labrador, Nova Scotia, or Prince Edward Island) where you'll be working. They must have a Confirmation of Designation from the province.

▪ The job must be full-time, meaning you'll work at least 30 paid hours per week.

▪ The job must be non-seasonal. In general, this means you have consistent and regularly scheduled paid employment throughout the year.

▪ The job is skill type/level 0, A or B under the NOC.

▪ The employer is offering you a job that will last for at least 1 year.

You must meet employment requirements for the job you are offered. You can find these requirements in the NOC. The job doesn't need to be in the same NOC as other jobs you've had.

10.3.1 When to Submit your Application

When you and the employer have completed all the steps, you can submit your application. To save time, start filling in your permanent resident application before all of the steps are completed. Gather the documents that go with your application as soon as you can. Check out the following site to learn more and download the forms needed for the application: Application for the Atlantic High-Skilled Program: www.canada.ca/en/immigration-refugees-citizenship/services/application/application-forms-guides/guide-5466-atlantic-immigration-pilot-program-atlantic-intermediate-skilled-program.html#5424E6 (short link: https://rb.gy/ueqxlk).

10.3.2. Frequently Asked Questions and Answers

My IELTS is ready and my ECA is being processed.

Question 1: Is there age limit for this program?

Question 2: Are we getting our PR through this process? If no, what do we need to do?

Answers:

1. There's no age limit.

2. Yes, after you get a job offer from a designated employer, you need to get a settlement plan. A settlement plan will help you and your family adjust to your new home in Atlantic Canada. It will provide you with useful resources and contacts to help you feel welcome in your new community. These plans are free, once you have your settlement plan, give a copy to your employer and keep a copy for yourself. If you're not in Canada, bring the plan with you when you move to Canada.

Get your **Certificate of Endorsement**: After you've your settlement plan, the province must endorse your job offer. Your employer will handle this process. Don't submit your permanent residence application until you confirm with the employer that your offer has been endorsed.

If the province endorses your job offer, you'll get a Certificate of Endorsement in the mail. Include your endorsement certificate with your permanent residence application along with other document needed for your PR application to IRCC via paper route, like ECA, POF, passports, IELTS, medical, PCC etc. including this endorsement certificate.

Question 3: How can I apply for jobs on the AIPP

Answers: Follow these steps:

1. Register with the job bank and search for openings here: www.jobbank.gc.ca/home.

2. Visit all the 4 Atlantic provinces' websites and download the designated employers.

3. Each province also has job portals. Explore it.

4. For designated employers, check LinkedIn pages for possible job openings and apply.

5. Endeavour to tailor your CV and cover letter to Canadian styles and send unsolicited application for job interests.

6. Apply widely.

7. Do not give up.

10.3.3. Additional Information

If you're looking how to get job offers, bookmark the following sites. Check frequently on them to know when is the next available virtual job fair, and register when registration opens again.

http://theworkroom.homestead.com/VJP.html (New Brunswick virtual job fair portal for outland applicants).

https://www.in-tac-expo.com/ (the largest virtual job fair in Canada).

Also contact the AIPP designated employers directly on their website or e-mail. Make sure your resume is tailored to Canadian standard. In your cover letter let the designated AIPP employer know that you fully meet the AIPP requirements and you have your IELTS scores and degree Evaluation report ready.

Below is a list of AIPP designated employers. Google the companies' names, go to their sites and apply directly or send e-mails to them.

https://www.jobscanadafair.com/Virtual-Job-Fair-Canada-s/1072.htm. Just register as a job seeker, so that you can see available jobs.

Nova Scotia AIPP designated employers

https://novascotiaimmigration.com/wp-content/uploads/Designated_AIP_employers.pdf

Prince Edward Island AIPP designated employers

https://www.princeedwardisland.ca/en/information/office-immigration/atlantic-immigration-pilot-designated-employers (short link: https://rb.gy/i5lppg).

Newfoundland and Labrador AIPP designated employers

https://www.gov.nl.ca/immigration/immigrating-to-newfoundland-and-labrador/atlantic-immigration-pilot-program/designated-employers/ (short link: https://rb.gy/of6r05).

New Brunswick AIPP designated employers

https://www.welcomenb.ca/content/dam/wel-bien/pdf/atlantic_immigration_pilot_project_designated_employers_list_april 2019.pdf (short link: https://rb.gy/ifwdyf).

10.3.4. Sample Cover Letters

Sample 1

Dear [insert hiring manager's name],

Regarding the [insert job title] position currently advertised on Monster.ca, please find attached a copy of my resume for your consideration.

Having worked within the industry for over [insert years experience], I have developed a wide range of skills that would meet, and exceed the expectations for the role. In my present role as a [insert your current job title] for [insert your current employer], I have had many achievements, including [insert your key achievement].

I would relish the opportunity to bring this level of success to your company. If you would like to get in touch to discuss my application and to arrange an interview, you can contact me via [insert your phone number or email address].

I look forward to hearing from you soon.

Yours sincerely, [insert your name]

Sample 2

Hiring Manager
421 Lahave Street,
Bridgewater, NS
B4V 3A2
Canada

Re: Assistant Manager of Customer Service & Operations (145441)

Dear Sir/Mam,

     I am interested in applying for the "Assistant Manager of Customer Service & Operations" job that was posted on your website on Dec 24, 2018. TJX' commitment to diversity and inclusion makes the organization stand out. I know that my international work experience makes me an outstanding candidate for this job. I am delighted we agree too!

     In this position, I would bring 14 years of sales, customer service, and staff management experience, mostly at multinationals. I have worked in very complex industries (B2C and B2B), including financial services and telecommunications. I am able to learn quickly about new products and upsell customers based on their needs. My colleagues would describe me as someone who can think outside the box and can achieve outstanding results with little directions. I strive to find new ways to solve problems!

     I am ready for a new career challenge and have been looking into relocating to Canada to join a large organization that is open to new ideas and that support self-starters. I would be grateful if you took a few minutes of your time to have a chat with me over the phone about the position. You will find that I am extremely hard-working and committed to my professional goals.

Warm regards,

Amin Dossani, B.Com.
Assistant Manager and Sales Representative

Figure 10.3.1: Sample cover letter 1

Jenny Job Seeker
20 Anywhere Street
Guysborough, Nova Scotia
B0H 1N0
(902) 555-5555

NOVA SCOTIA WORKS

April 3, 2017

Mr. John Smith
Director of Human Resources
Call Centre
123 Main Street
Antigonish, Nova Scotia
B2G 2R8

Re: **Sales Representative Position**

Dear Mr. Smith:

In response to your recent advertisement, I would like to be considered for the position of Sales Representative.

During the past ten years, I have been employed as a Customer Service Representative at Clothes to You Inc., where I supervised and developed personnel and assisted in the facilitation of daily operations. In addition, I have been involved in a number of diverse employment situations, including a self-owned business, in which I successfully utilized various sales techniques, including cold calling, telemarketing and prospecting. As my resume indicates, I have accumulated several years of experience in the development of marketing and sales strategies.

I would enjoy being a part your team and I am available for an interview at your convenience. You may contact me at (902) 555-5555. Thank you in advance for your time and consideration.

Sincerely,

Canada   NOVA SCOTIA   Career
                         CONNECTIONS

Jenny Job Seeker

Nova Scotia Works Employment Services Centres

information@careerconnections.ca

Figure 10.3.2: Sample cover letter 2

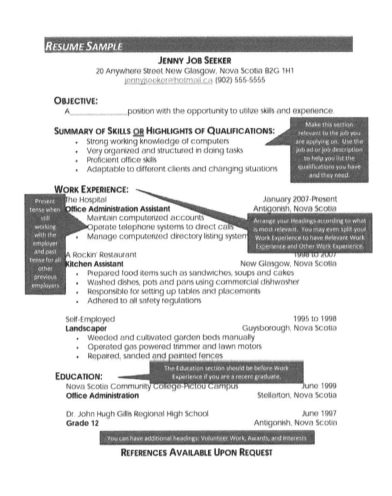

Figure 10.3.3: A resume sample

If you need further help in your application, don't hesitate to use my support link at the bottom of this book. I will get back to you very quickly.

11. Provincial Nomination Program (PNP)

There are 11 Canadian provinces. Each PNP has its own criteria for selection and invitation. If you do not have a job offer, you can't get PNP from some of the provinces. Below are a few facts you must know about PNP. You can search Google for more.

11.1. Facts about PNP

1. Alberta

You have to be present in Alberta to apply, or at least you have studied there or you have your close relatives living there. They pick directly from Express Entry pool. It's a system that was launched in June 2018. You do not need to apply directly. The province sends you a notification of interest to your EE profile. They pick directly from EE pool, preference is given to those having a close connection to the province. But at times even regular applicants get an NOI.

2. Manitoba

If you read about Manitoba, you may be already qualified for that but they have bizarre condition of having compulsory close relative residing there, i.e., a strong connection. If you have a close friend there, it may give you 50 points but it will not be sufficient to get invited so if you don't have any connection in Manitoba, you need to have a job offer. it makes everything easier.

3. PEI Prince Edward Island

They do not have clear rules on who they will invite. Generally, you need to have an EE profile to apply for Expression of Interest. If you have an active EE profile just go to PEI website and apply. A general assumption is that they invite as per their labor market requirements. The sad fact is that they have not invited anyone from outside Canada so far. So, it appears there's no chance there. If you must, just apply and forget about it.

4. New Brunswick

You need to have an EE profile first. It's a hide-and-seek PNP. It opens and closes for receiving applications throughout the year. Generally, if you have job offer or connection to the province, just be ready to submit your EOI profile all the time. They also have an option to submit without job offer or connection but you should have attended their information session that they organize throughout the year in several parts of the world.

If you manage to attend any of these sessions, you will be eligible to apply. They also have an occupation in demand (OID) list, a list of occupations the province finds desirable. If your occupation referred to as NOC is in their OID list, then you can apply. This stream opens 1 or 2 times a year.

5. Ontario

No specific guidelines. They pick directly from the EE pool as per their changing labor market requirements in Ontario. If you are an I.T. person and if you have 430+ CRS points, you have fair chances to get picked directly from the EE pool. Another option is French language ability. If you have an active EE profile and CRS points around 300–350 or anything above, and you have French language credentials, you'd likely be invited. This is happening at the moment but we do not know when it will stop.

6. Saskatchewan

It's by far the most popular PNP for outsiders who do not have job offers. It's still open. Apply directly on the website for your Expression of interest submission. Your NOC must be in their Occupation in Demand (OID).

They have 2 streams, OID and Express Entry. Previously if you score 60 points as per SINP points grid system, you had a fair chance of nomination but the system has changed now. You need to compete now with other applicants in EOI pool (Expression of Interest).

In Express Entry, you must have an EE profile. CRS points alone do not matter. If you score a minimum of 60 as per SINP points grid, you may apply.

In OID, you do not need to have an EE profile: CLB 4 will get you eligible to apply for OID but you still need to score that 60 points grids.

You will need to create an account for Expression of Interest system. You will be ranked among all applicants in the pool. Those who got higher points will be invited. In this case it's very obvious that those who are already in Saskatchewan or with strong connections will get higher points.

7. Nova Scotia

By far the best and friendliest PNP. The drawback is they have very limited OID list. You need to have an EE profile first to be eligible to apply for category B (without job offers) and your NOC should be there to apply. You need to score 67 points in order to qualify. Just go to NS website and you will find the application guide there which is very simple to understand. They open intake throughout the year and take limited applications. It's first come, first served basis. So, when the intake opens, it's very hard to apply because of website traffic.

8. Newfoundland

By default, this is not everyone's choice, but you need EE profile and job offer.

11.2. Application Process Using 4 Case Studies

11.2.1. Case Study 1: Manitoba

The MPNP (Manitoba PNP) for Skilled Workers is locally driven and based on the needs of Manitoba employers. We select internationally trained and experienced workers who have the skills needed in the local labor market, and nominate them to receive Canadian permanent resident visas to settle and work in Manitoba.

The MPNP for Skilled Workers Overseas nominates applicants who demonstrate an established connection to Manitoba through:

• The support of family members or friends;

• Previous education or work experience in the province; or

• Through an Invitation to Apply received directly from the MPNP as part of a Strategic Recruitment Initiative.

In other words, you need a family member who is a Citizen of Canada or a Permanent Resident to sponsor you.

11.2.2. Case Study 2: Alberta

You have to be present in Alberta to apply, or at least you have studied there, or you have your close relatives living there. They pick directly from Express Entry pool. It's a system that was launched in June 2018. You do not need to apply directly. The province sends you a notification of interest to your EE profile.

They pick directly from EE pool, preference is given to those having a close connection to the province. But at times even regular applicants get an NOI.

11.2.3. Case Study 3: Prince Edward Island

Till date, No one from outside Canada has been nominated yet. Only people who live in Canada but are not citizens or PR holders have been nominated. So, if you're going to Canada for school or for any other reason, this might be a good province to apply to for PR.

11.2.4. Case Study 5 New Brunswick:

You need to have an EE profile first. Some call it the Hide-and-seek PNP. It opens and closes for receiving applications throughout the year without any notice. Generally, if you know French, or have job offer or connection to the province, just be ready to submit your EOI profile all the time.

They also have an option to submit without job offer or connection but you should have attended their information session that they organize throughout the year in several parts of the world. If you manage to attend any of these sessions, you will be eligible to apply. This stream opens 1 or 2 times a year.

11.3. Provincial Official Websites

1) British Columbia: www.welcomebc.ca/

2) Alberta: www.alberta.ca/index.aspx

3) Manitoba: www.immigratemanitoba.com/

4) Ontario: www.ontario.ca/page/getting-settled-ontario

5) Nunavut: www.gov.nu.ca/

6) Prince Edward Island: www.princeedwardisland.ca/en

7) New Brunswick: www.welcomenb.ca/content/wel-bien/en.html

8) Nova Scotia: www.novascotiaimmigration.com/

9) Newfoundland and Labrador: www.gov.nl.ca/immigration/

10) Yukon: www.immigration.gov.yk.ca/

11) Northwest Territories: www.gov.nt.ca/

12) Quebec: www.immigrationquebec.gouv.qc.ca

If you need further help in your application, don't hesitate to use my support link at the bottom of this book. I will get back to you very quickly.

12. Rural & Northern Immigration Pilot Program (RNIP)

The aim of this pilot is to support middle class jobs in rural and northern communities. Increasing levels of youth out-migration, declining fertility rates, and lower levels of immigration have drastically reduced the talent pool of these communities. The story is different in larger urban centers.

Since communities will be responsible for candidate recruitment and endorsement for permanent residence, interested candidates should start connecting with the key actors in these communities, research opportunities and prepare accordingly. This will also help to manage expectations.

If I were a candidate, by now, I would have researched which organization(s) sponsored the application of the community that I am interested in and start reaching out already e.g., Economic Development Organizations, Chambers of Commerce, Employment Agencies, the Municipality, etc., and even potential employers.

Don't forget that each community can nominate 250 candidates annually. That may sound like a lot but pales into insignificance if you take into consideration that applicants would be applying from around the world, including from within Canada. I can tell you that these participating communities have already been flooded with expressions of interest and enquiries.

From my research, Northern Ontario, where 5 of these communities are from, have skills shortages in the following occupations:

1. Personal support workers

2. Doctors

3. Skilled trades (Carpenters, Millwrights, Mechanics, Industrial Electricians, Machinists, HVAC, Ironworkers, Bricklayers, Electricians, Fitter/Welders and Plumbers)

4. Truck drivers

5. Retail trade personnel

6. Hospitality and tourism

7. Nurses

Please note that the above list is not intended to be exhaustive and labor needs can vary from one community to another.

RNIP is designed to bring economic development in the Rural and northern areas of Canada. Various communities have been selected to participate. They include:

Ontario
Thunder Bay
Sault Ste. Marie
Sudbury
Timmins
North Bay

Manitoba
Gretna-Rhineland-Altona-Plum Coulee
Brandon

Saskatchewan
Moose Jaw

Alberta
Claresholm

British Columbia
West Kootenay
Vernon

12.1. Official website of Participating Communities

Sault Ste. Marie: www.sault-canada.com/en/

Thunder Bay: www.thunderbay.ca/en/CEDC.aspx

Timmins: www.timminsedc.com/

North Bay: www.nbdcc.ca/

Moose Jaw: www.mjchamber.com/

Central Kootenay: www.futuresbc.com/

Sudbury: www.investsudbury.ca/about-us/

North Okanagan: www.futuresbc.com/

Claresholm: www.claresholm.ca/contact-directory/department-directory/economic-development

Brandon: www.economicdevelopmentbrandon.com/immigration-resources

Gretna-Rhineland-Altona-Plum Coulee: www.seedrpga.com/immigration-pilot

RNIP is a little similar to the AIPP in the sense that its requirements are a little relaxed compared to the Federal Skilled Worker. Here, CLB 4 and above is adequate depending on your skill type. Skill type C and D can get in with CLB 4, skill type B can get in with CLB 5 and skill type 0 and A can get in with CLB 6.

Proof of Fund for this program is also a little relaxed. You need only CAD 8,000 for one person and this is a significant reduction in the figures stipulated for other programs like the FSW and FST.

You also do not need a degree for this. Although, you must have your high school (secondary school) certificates. Some of these cities started their immigration program on December 1, 2019 while others were yet to commence processing. For those that had started, it was expected successful applicants would start arriving the communities by 2020.

The communities that have started their programs so far have all indicated that job offers are an important part of the application process. Basically, the summary of the process is that you find a job in a community, write to the authorities, they will endorse your permanent Residence application, and with this, you can obtain your PR at the federal level. Some of the communities will be working with their community developments and Chambers of commerce in this process.

12.2. How to Apply

To apply to any of these, you'll need…

1. Education Credential Assessment

2. IELTS (from CLB 4 and above)

3. Reference letter from your CURRENT job (yes, your current job. Employers will be looking at what you are currently doing and what you can offer them.)

4. Update your CV to Canadian format. Maintain your contact. Make it look authentic, as it's the only means of them knowing your credibility.

5. Prepare your POF (Proof of Funds).

6. Choose your communities and make research. Make research. This cannot be over emphasized.

12.2.1. Steps to Apply for PR

There are 4 steps to applying for permanent residence under this pilot.

1. Check that you meet both

- IRCC eligibility requirements (https://www.canada.ca/en/immigration-refugees-citizenship/services/immigrate-canada/rural-northern-immigration-pilot/pr-eligibility.html - Short link: https://rb.gy/uurcgt) and

- The community-specific requirements (https://www.canada.ca/en/immigration-refugees-citizenship/services/immigrate-canada/rural-northern-immigration-pilot/pr-eligibility.html#community – short link: https://rb.gy/s0do1z).

2. Find an eligible job with an employer in one of the participating communities.

3. Once you have a job offer, submit your application for recommendation to the community.

4. If a community recommends you, apply for permanent residence.

Each community will also have its own

• Additional eligibility requirements.

• Job search process.

• Community recommendation application process.

This information will be available on its website.

What you can expect from a community

This pilot is community-driven, meaning the communities will

• Assess prospective candidates who

  • Best fit the economic needs of these community

  • Have a genuine employment opportunity that meets their community requirements

  • Have the intention of staying in the community

• Recommend candidates for permanent residence to IRCC for a final decision.

• Connect newcomers with settlement services and mentoring opportunities with established members of the community.

Now, let's talk about some of these communities and their requirements (case studies).

12.3. Application Process Using 2 Case Studies

12.3.1. Case Study 1: Altona/Rhineland, MB

First you must meet the federal requirements, then meet the specific requirements of this community.

You need to secure a job. Click on this link to see available job listing: www.northstarats.com/SEED.

If you do not find a job posting that meets your work experience and/or education, I encourage you to create a candidate profile which offers the option to set up career alert(s) automatically notifying you by email of job opportunities matching your criteria, as they become available.

A complete resume is required when applying for a position. The key components of a complete resume consist of:

• Your name and contact information

• Full education history

• Full work history

• Skills and Activities are optional

• Three references (preferably work related)

Please click this short link to open a sample template that may be used to create your own resume: https://rb.gy/7dz9k2.

Other Community Specific Requirements:

1. Candidate must intend to live within the boundaries (as defined in the Ministerial Instructions: https://canadagazette.gc.ca/rp-pr/p1/2019/2019-08-17/html/notice-avis-eng.html) of the Town of Altona or Municipality of Rhineland.

2. Only a Candidate who has successfully created a "Candidate Profile" on https://www.seedrpga.com/immigration-pilot will be able to apply for qualified job postings through the Rural and Northern Immigration Pilot.

3. Only qualified positions by employers located within the boundaries of the Town of Altona or Municipality of Rhineland (as defined in the Ministerial Instructions) that meet the Employment Requirements (as defined in the Ministerial Instructions section two (2)) will be posted on https://www.seedrpga.com/immigration-pilot

4. Qualified positions must also be posted on www.jobbank.gc.ca and/or www.localjobshop.ca/.

Therefore, any job you secure that isn't posted on these sites will not be acceptable.

Altona/Rhineland Comprehensive Priority Points Grid

The Vetting Committee will assess the eligibility of every candidate who applies for community recommendation taking into consideration the priority factors outlined in the Comprehensive Priority Points Grid. The top-ranking candidates will move onto further assessment including an applicant interview to ensure they intend to reside in the community.

a. Candidate has received a qualifying job offer in the sector of Agriculture and Manufacturing

Yes +20.

b. Candidate has received a qualifying job offer in the sector of Construction, Food Processing and Financial Services

Yes +10.

c. The job offer is from an established employer who has been operating a business within the boundaries (as defined in the Ministerial Instructions) of the Town of Altona or Municipality of Rhineland for a minimum of ten (10) years, or with a business that has invested a minimum of $250,000 capital within the boundaries (as defined in the Ministerial Instructions) of the Town of Altona or Municipality of Rhineland

Yes +10.

d. The job offer is from an employer who will provide the candidate with a workplace mentor for a minimum of six (6) months

Yes +5.

e. Job offer is in National Occupational Classification (NOC) skills NOC A, NOC B: +10

or NOC Yes +5.

f. Candidate possess a valid driver's license from country of origin

Yes +5.

g. Candidate has lived as an adult (18 years of age or older) in a community with a population of 10,000 people or less, and located one (1) hour (travel distance) away from a large and densely populated urban area for a minimum of six (6) months

Yes +5.

h. Candidate has a family member and/or friend who is a permanent resident of Canada or a Canadian citizen and has been living within the boundaries (as defined in the Ministerial Instructions) of the Town of Altona and/or Municipality of Rhineland for a minimum of two (2) years.

Parents, siblings or children: +20.

Friend, grandparent, uncle, aunt, cousin, niece or nephew: +10.

i. Candidate has previously spent one (1) week or more within the boundaries (as defined in the Ministerial Instructions) of the Town of Altona and/or Municipality of Rhineland

Yes +5.

j. The candidate has a spouse/common-law-partner with work experience that could fill labour needs in the following industry sectors: Agriculture, Construction, Education, Financial Services, Food Processing, Pharmaceuticals, Healthcare/Hospital, Manufacturing, Social Services, Retail, Technology, Transportation

Yes +10.

k. The candidate has a spouse/common-law-partner with post-secondary education that could fill labor needs in the following industry sectors: Agriculture, Construction, Education, Financial Services, Food Processing,

Pharmaceuticals, Healthcare/Hospital, Manufacturing, Social Services, Retail, Technology, Transportation

Yes +10.

l. The candidate is between the ages of 25 to 38 years old as of the date the application for recommendation is received by SEED

Yes +10.

Additional Information

It's the applicant's responsibility to provide documentation that confirms that the factors are met. Applicants who are claiming points for a family member or friend within Altona/Rhineland must provide a verification letter including the name, relationship, and contact information for their family member or friend. SEED may contact this individual as part of the assessment of your application.

Applicants who are claiming points for a spouse or common-law partner's work experience, must provide a resume detailing their past work experience including the name of the employer, the job title and main duties, the dates the position was held, and a reference who could confirm the work experience. SEED may contact the reference as part of the assessment of your application.

Applicants who are claiming points for a spouse or common-law partner's education, must provide a copy of the degree, certificate, or diploma. SEED may request additional information/documentation to validate the information provided in your application for recommendation.

12.3.2. Case Study 2: Brandon, MB

The Federal Requirements remain the same.

Specific Community Recommendation Application Process

1. Foreign National creates an online candidate profile at BrandonRNIP site here: www.northstarats.com/Brandon-RNIP. Foreign National uploads any relevant documents they wish to include in the profile such as, but not limited to, English language resume / curriculum vitae, IRCC recognized language test results, education credential assessments, letters of reference, etc.

2. Foreign National applies for jobs located within the Brandon RNIP boundaries (Brandon and a 55 km radius of Brandon). All jobs posted at BrandonRNIP site are confirmed as eligible for the Brandon RNIP. If a job is not posted on the Brandon RNIP website, it means the job has not yet been screened by the Economic Development Office (EDB) to ensure it meets Brandon RNIP eligibility criteria, and therefore would not be a qualifying job. Employers can contact the Economic Development office to schedule a job-screening meeting to determine if their job vacancy is eligible for the Brandon RNIP.

A complete resume is required when applying for a position. Supplying a cover letter in addition to your resume when applying for a job is highly recommended. The cover letter introduces you to the company and should contain information that motivates the reader to review your resume.

At a minimum, the following information should be included in your resume:

• Your full name and contact information (phone and e-mail).

• Full education history.

• Full work history (including a brief description of the duties you did while employed at the listed job).

• Highlighting your skills and personal interests are optional.

• Three references (preferably work related) which include name, position, phone number including country code and email address.

If you do not have a resume, please click the following link to open a resume template that you can use to create a resume, or search online for other templates: www.economicdevelopmentbrandon.com/images/RNIP/Resume_Template.docx.

EDB reviews applications for employment received through the Brandon RNIP website and only forwards the applications that meet minimum skills, education and experience requirements to the employer who has the posted job vacancy.

Please note that if a Foreign National regularly applies for jobs posted on the Brandon RNIP website for which they do not possess the mandatory skills, experience or education, all future job applications submitted through the Brandon RNIP website will be considered ineligible and will not be sent onto employers for consideration.

3. Foreign National undergoes the employer screening process when invited to do so by the employer offering a Brandon RNIP qualifying job opportunity: www.canada.ca/en/immigration-refugees-citizenship/services/immigrate-canada/rural-northern-immigration-pilot/community-partners.html (short link: https://rb.gy/d3rvd3).

4. Foreign National receives a qualifying job offer from employer on IRCC form IMM5984: www.canada.ca/content/dam/ircc/documents/pdf/english/kits/forms/imm5984 e.pdf.

5. Foreign National in receipt of the qualifying job offer applies to the Brandon RNIP for a Community Recommendation, on IRCC form IMM 5911 via the process established by EDB: www.canada.ca/content/dam/ircc/documents/pdf/english/kits/forms/imm5911 e.pdf.

6. Foreign National supplies EDB with requested documents and information to ensure a complete Community Recommendation application has been received by EDB.

7. The Economic Development office reviews the Foreign National's Community Recommendation application against federal mandatory eligibility criteria and Community Recommendation prioritization criteria, assigning points as applicable. The top-ranking candidates will undergo further assessment including an applicant interview (through a form of video conferencing) to confirm the applicant's intent to reside in the community.

8. Only a monthly basis, the Brandon RNIP Recommendation Committee reviews the highest scoring Community Recommendation applications and makes one of three decisions listed below:

a. Approve Community Recommendation

b. Place the Community Recommendation on hold

c. Decline to issue a Community Recommendation

Community Recommendation applications placed on hold will remain under consideration for up to six consecutive months from the date of application. While on hold the application will be considered for Community Recommendation in each of the monthly assessment periods occurring during the consideration period.

At the end of 6 months, the application will no longer be under consideration. At this time, the employer who originally provided the qualifying job offer may wish to issue a new job offer, or the candidate may secure a new job offer for a different position posted on

Economic Development Brandon's website. Either of these options requires the applicant to submit an updated application for recommendation.

Typically, Brandon will limit monthly community recommendations to approximately 10% of the annual recommendations allocated by Immigration, Refugees and Citizenship Canada.

9. The Foreign National and employer providing the qualifying job offer are advised of the Brandon RNIP Recommendation Committee's decision regarding their application for

Community Recommendation. If the Foreign National receives a Brandon RNIP Community Recommendation, the Economic Development office completes the federally provided recommendation form and provides the recommendation to the applicant.

10. The Foreign National submits a complete permanent resident application to Immigration, Refugees and Citizenship Canada (IRCC) through the RNIP immigration program: www.canada.ca/en/immigration-refugees-citizenship/services/application/application-forms-guides/application-rural-northern-immigration.html.

Brandon's Community Recommendation must accompany the application. The application for permanent residence must be submitted within 6 months of the date that appears on the Community Recommendation.

11. IRCC confirms the permanent resident application is complete or returns the application to the Foreign National to provide missing documents and/or information. Once a complete application is received, IRRC assesses the permanent resident application as per their normal review process.

12. The Foreign National receives confirmation from IRCC that a complete Permanent Residence Application has been received. At this time, if the employer and Foreign National desire, a temporary foreign worker application can be made through the normal channels: https://www.canada.ca/en/immigration-refugees-citizenship/services/work-canada/permit/temporary.html. Temporary worker approval allows the individual (and their family if desired) to come to Brandon, Manitoba, Canada and work while they are waiting for a decision on their permanent resident application.

13. The Foreign National and family (if applicable), begin life in Brandon once the Brandon RNIP applicant's temporary worker permit is approved or their permanent resident application is approved (whichever occurs first) and Canada Border Customs Agency approves the Foreign National's entry to Canada. The employer and community connect the newcomer and their family (if applicable) with services and community connections to support their settlement.

If you need further help in your application, don't hesitate to use my support link at the bottom of this book. I will get back to you very quickly.

13. Caregiver Program

As a caregiver, you have options to come to Canada to become a permanent resident or work temporarily.

13.1. Program Checklist

1) **Get an Offer of Employment** - as either a Home Child Care Provider or a Home Support Worker. There is currently a huge vacancy in the home care provision industry. For example, the British Colombia Care Providers Association projects 2,800 vacant jobs in senior care over five years. (British Colombia is one of the ten provinces in Canada). LISTEN: BCCPA outlines seniors care labor shortage concerns: https://omny.fm/shows/cknw/the-seniors-care-labour-shortage.

2) **Get your Educational Credential Evaluated**. The educational requirement is just a one-year post-secondary education credential or higher. An ECA is used to check that your completed educational credential is valid and equal to a completed Canadian one-year post-secondary education credential or higher.

3) **Earning a CLB 5 in your IELTS Exam**. As stated earlier, the good news with this route to Canada is that you do not need to be a genius in English. Getting a CLB 9 or 10 as required for express entry can remain a dream, but trust me getting a CLB 5 is a walk in the park.

4) **Getting your Medical Report and Police Certificate**. This is country-specific.

What you need to know is what hospitals are accredited by the Immigration Refugees and Citizenship Canada (IRCC) for medical evaluation. Also getting a police report from your country should be straight-forward

5) **Submitting a Work Permit Application and a Permanent Residence Application**. Once you have your offer of employment, ECA report, IELTS, Medical report, and Police Certificate, you can now begin your Work Permit

and PR application. You can apply along with your spouse and children (if applicable).

6) **After submitting a Work Permit Application and a Permanent Residence Application** - how do you track the status? If your application is successful, you will get an email requesting you to complete Biometrics at any Visa Application Centre (VAC), e.g., VFS.

7) **Preparing for life in Canada**.

8) **Applying for your Permanent Residence**. After getting 24 months of work experience as either a home childcare worker or home support worker, you can apply for permanent residence.

13.2. Permanent Residence for Caregivers

13.2.1. Home Child Care Provider Pilot and Home Support Worker Pilot

As of June 18, 2019, you may be able to apply for permanent residence through the Home Child Care Provider Pilot or Home Support Worker Pilot (https://www.canada.ca/en/immigration-refugees-citizenship/services/immigrate-canada/caregivers/child-care-home-support-worker.html) if you:

▪ Meet the eligibility requirements, and

▪ Have a job offer to work in one of these occupations.

Through these pilots, you'll get an open work permit to come to Canada and work temporarily. This work permit:

▪ Is occupation-restricted (so you have to work in that specific occupation).

▪ Doesn't need a Labor Market Impact Assessment (LMIA).

▪ Lets you get the work experience you need to be eligible for permanent residence.

If you recently worked as a home childcare provider or support worker, your experience may count towards your eligibility for permanent residence.

Temporary work for caregivers

If you don't meet the requirements for permanent residence as a caregiver, you may be able to work temporarily.

Applying to extend your work permit

If you're currently working in Canada as a caregiver, you may be eligible to extend your work permit through the Temporary Foreign Worker Program (TFWP). Your employer will need to get a positive Labour Market Impact Assessment (LMIA) first: https://www.canada.ca/en/employment-social-development/services/foreign-workers/caregiver/apply.html.

The Home Child Care Provider Pilot and the Home Support Worker Pilot are 5-year pilot programs that let qualified caregivers and their family members come to Canada with the goal of becoming permanent residents.

If you've been offered a job in Canada as a caregiver or have experience working in Canada as a caregiver, you may be able to apply for permanent residence through one of these pilots.

The application process will be different depending on your situation and how much qualifying work experience you have. For effective job search, please note that these jobs are sometimes referred to as;

- Personal Support Worker - PSW

- Health Care Aide - HCA

- Developmental Support Worker - DSW

- Community Support Worker - CSW

- Nursing Assistant - NA

- Caregiver (Informal)

Qualifying work experience

Qualifying work experience means you've worked full-time in Canada in one of these National Occupational Classification (NOC) jobs:

• Home child care provider - NOC 4411 (https://www.immigration.ca/national-occupational-classification-noc-4411-home-child-care-providers)

- Experience as a foster parent doesn't count

or

• Home support worker - NOC 4412 (https://www.immigration.ca/noc-4412-home-support-workers-housekeepers-related-occupations)

- Experience as a housekeeper doesn't count

Your level of work experience determines how you should apply for the Caregiver Program.

As an applicant, you fall under one of these categories:

1. You don't have any qualifying work experience

2. You have some work experience but less than 2 years

3. In the last 3 years, you've worked for at least 2 years as a full-time care giver (remember, your experience as a foster parent or housekeeper doesn't count).

Category 1: You don't have any qualifying work experience

If you don't have any qualifying work experience, you can apply for permanent residence through the Home Child Care Provider Pilot or the Home Support Worker Pilot as long as you meet the other eligibility requirements.

How the process works:

1. You apply to either the Home Child Care Provider Pilot or the Home Support Worker Pilot, depending on which occupation you plan to work in.

2. You submit a work permit application together with your permanent residence application.

3. If you meet the requirements, you get a work permit to work in Canada temporarily.

4. The work permit you get is an occupation-restricted open work permit and lets you work as a caregiver for any employer.

5. Get at least 24 months of work experience to qualify for permanent residence.

6. You send us proof of your work experience once you have enough.

7. We make a final decision on your application for permanent residence.

Family members

Your family members are also eligible to come with you to Canada. If they want to work or study while in Canada, you can include their work permit (https://www.canada.ca/en/immigration-refugees-citizenship/services/work-canada/permit/temporary/work-permit.html) or study permit (https://www.canada.ca/en/immigration-refugees-citizenship/services/study-canada/study-permit.html) applications with your application.

Category 2: You have some work experience but less than 2 years

If you have some qualifying work experience, but less than 24 months, you can apply for the Home Child Care Provider Pilot or the Home Support Worker Pilot, as long as you meet the other eligibility requirements.

How the process works:

1. You apply to either the Home Child Care Provider Pilot or the Home Support Worker Pilot, depending on which occupation you plan to work in.

2. You submit a work permit application together with your permanent residence application.

3. If you meet the requirements, you get a work permit to work in Canada temporarily.

4. The work permit you get is an occupation-restricted open work permit and lets you work as a caregiver for any employer.

5. Get at least 24 months of work experience to qualify for permanent residence.

6. You send proof of your work experience once you have enough.

7. A final decision is made on your application for permanent residence.

Family members

Your family members are also eligible to come with you to Canada. If they want to work or study while in Canada, you can include their work or study permit applications with your application.

Category 3: In the last 3 years, you've worked for at least 2 years as a full-time care giver

If you already have 24 months of qualifying work experience, you and your family members may be eligible to apply for permanent residence through the Home Child Care Provider Pilot or the Home Support Worker Pilot. When you apply, you need to include documents to prove you have enough qualifying work experience.

Eligibility

You may be eligible to apply for the Home Child Care Provider Pilot or Home Support Worker Pilot, if you:

- Have a genuine and valid job offer

- Are able to do the job

- Meet the language level

- Meet the education requirement

- Are admissible to Canada

- Plan to live outside the province of Quebec as a permanent resident

Genuine and valid job offer

The job you're offered must be:

- Made using Offer of Employment IMM 5983 (PDF, 2.33 MB): https://www.canada.ca/content/dam/ircc/documents/pdf/english/kits/forms/imm5983e.pdf.

- Full-time, which means at least 30 hours of paid work each week.

- From a Canadian employer.

- Outside the province of Quebec.

- From an employer who's not an embassy, high commission or consulate.

- Genuine, meaning there's a real need to hire you.

The job you're offered must be in the National Occupational Classification (NOC) job that matches the pilot you apply for:

Home childcare provider (NOC 4411)

- You must care for children under the age of 18 in your own home or in your employer's home.

- You don't need to live in your employer's home to qualify.

- Experience as a foster parent doesn't count.

Home support worker (NOC 4412)

- You must care for someone who needs help from a home support worker

- either in your own home or in your employer's home

- You don't need to live in your employer's home to qualify

- Only home support workers are eligible under NOC 4412

- Experience as a housekeeper doesn't count

If you have any work experience, your qualifying work experience must be in one of these jobs. It cannot be a mix of both jobs. Make sure the job you're offered matches the work experience you already have.

Ability to do the work

We use any past experience or training you have to decide if you're able to do the work described in the NOC job description (lead statement).

Language levels

You need to take a language test to prove you meet the minimum language skills.

To measure your English or French skills, these are used:

- Canadian Language Benchmarks (CLB) for English.

- Niveaux de compétence linguistique canadien (NCLC) for French.

The minimum language skill is CLB 5 in English or NLCL 5 in French for all 4 language skills:

- Writing

- Reading

- Listening

- Speaking

Education

You must have a completed post-secondary education credential of at least 1 year in Canada. If you don't have a Canadian education credential, you need to get your foreign education credential assessed to show that it's equal to a completed Canadian post-secondary education credential of at least one year. Examples of such post-secondary school credentials include your Diplomas, a course on Care giving or Child caregiving, etc.

13.3. How to Apply Step by Step

Step 1: Get a valid job offer

You need a genuine and valid job offer before you apply. The person who wants to hire you needs to give you the completed Offer of Employment IMM 5983 (PDF, 2.23 MB) for you to sign and include in your application: https://www.canada.ca/content/dam/ircc/documents/pdf/english/kits/forms/imm5983e.pdf.

Step 2: Get the instruction guide

Applying from outside Canada.

Use the instruction guide on the following for applicants outside Canada to get the forms you need and to help you fill out the forms correctly:

https://www.canada.ca/en/immigration-refugees-citizenship/services/application/application-forms-guides/guide-0104-home-care-support/tr-overseas.html (short link: https://rb.gy/qfiewh).

Step 3: Complete your application

1. Fill out the forms on a computer.

2. Some forms have a 'Validate' button that helps you check if you completed all the fields in the form. When you're done filling out these forms, click 'Validate'. If there are any fields you still need to fill out, they'll be outlined in red.

3. After you successfully validate the forms, you'll get a barcode page

4. Print out all the forms, including the barcode pages

5. Sign and date all forms

6. Use the Document Checklist – Home Child Care Provider and Home Support Worker [IMM 5981] (PDF, 3.39 MB) to make sure you have everything:
https://www.canada.ca/content/dam/ircc/documents/pdf/english/kits/forms/imm5981e.pdf.

Answer all questions carefully, completely and truthfully. There are serious consequences if you misrepresent yourself or leave out relevant information on your application.

Step 4: Pay your application fees

In most cases, your fees include:

• Processing fees for you and anyone you include on your application for permanent residence

• The Right of Permanent Residence Fee (RPRF):
https://www.cic.gc.ca/english/information/fees/fees.asp#rprf.

• Work permit processing fee and open work permit holder fee

• Biometrics fee: https://www.canada.ca/en/immigration-refugees-citizenship/campaigns/biometrics/facts.html.

Study and work permit fees for your family members

If your family members are applying for study or work permits with your application, you need to pay fees for those too. When you finish paying your fees, you must print a receipt for each of your payments and include all your receipts with your application. You have to pay your fees online: https://www.cic.gc.ca/english/information/fees/index.asp.

Biometrics

You and your family members may need to give your fingerprints and photograph (biometric information) at a biometric collection service point. In most cases, you must pay a biometrics fee when you submit your application. Otherwise, you may experience delays. The biometrics fee covers the cost of collecting fingerprints and a digital photo.

After you pay the biometrics fee with a complete application, we'll send you a letter to tell you if you need to give your biometrics and where you can go. You must show this letter when you give your biometrics. You must give your biometrics in person. You should book an appointment. Find out here if you need to give biometrics: https://www.cic.gc.ca/english/visit/biometrics.asp.

Third-party fees

You have to pay third parties if you need a:

• Medical exam,

• Police certificate,

• Language test, or

• Educational Credential Assessment.

The instruction guide can help you understand which fees apply to you and how to pay them.

Step 5: Submit your application

Make sure you:

• Answer all questions,

• Sign your application and all forms,

• Include your fee payment receipt, and

• Include all the supporting documents.

Before you submit your application, use the Document Checklist – Home Child Care Provider and Home Support Worker [IMM 5981] (PDF, 3.39 MB) to make sure you don't forget anything. If you forget something, your application will be sent back to you. Mail your complete application to the appropriate address at the Case Processing Centre in Edmonton, Alberta, Canada.

Don't send your application to any other processing center or immigration office.

Biometrics

If you have to give biometrics, we send you a biometric instruction letter (BIL) which will direct you to a list of biometric collection service points you may choose from. You must bring the BIL with you to the biometric collection service point to give your biometrics.

Processing your application

An immigration officer will make sure that you:

• Filled out your application forms correctly and signed them,

• Paid your fees,

• Submitted your biometrics (if required),

• Submitted proof of qualifying work experience,

• Meet the language requirements,

• Meet the education requirements, and

• Included all other required documents and information specified in the application package.

If your application isn't complete, it won't be processed and will be sent back to you.

Your application will be delayed if:

• There is criminal or security problems or more background checks need to be done.

• Your family situation is not clear – reasons could include a divorce or an adoption that is not yet complete or child custody issues that have not been resolved, or

• The processing office has to contact other IRCC offices in Canada or abroad to verify the data you gave.

You can check the status of your application online after the processing of your application has started: https://services3.cic.gc.ca/ecas/introduction.do?app=ecas.

While your application is in process, you must tell the processing office if you've changed your address (https://www.canada.ca/en/immigration-refugees-citizenship/services/application/change-address.html) or contact information (https://www.cic.gc.ca/english/contacts/web-form.asp).

Decision on your application

A decision on your application is made based on:

• Whether you meet the eligibility criteria (https://www.canada.ca/en/immigration-refugees-citizenship/services/immigrate-canada/caregivers/child-care-home-support-worker/complete-experience-eligibility.html (short link: https://rb.gy/6yvsrf)),

• If you submitted a complete application, and

• If you are admissible to Canada.

You'll be contacted you if you need to send more documents, or if you're approved for permanent residence.

Confirmation of permanent residence

If your application for permanent residence is approved, you'll be asked to send your passport to the processing office so they can issue your permanent resident visa. This visa includes your Confirmation of Permanent Residence (COPR) and, if you need one to enter Canada, an entry visa.

Your COPR will have information about who you are as well as your photograph. Check to make sure it's correct. It should be the same as the information on your passport. If there is a mistake on your COPR, contact them: https://www.cic.gc.ca/english/contacts/web-form.asp.

If you're already in Canada…

When your application for permanent residence is approved, you'll be contacted. They'll let you know what to do next. You'll have to do a short interview with an immigration officer. You have 2 options for your interview:

• Make an appointment at one of our offices in Canada (https://www.canada.ca/en/immigration-refugees-citizenship/corporate/contact-ircc/offices/canada-appointment-only.html). This is the best option because you won't have to leave and re-enter Canada.

• Go to a Canadian "port of entry" (border crossing) and bring your COPR and your permanent resident visa (if they gave you one).

During the interview, the officer will:

• Make sure all your documents are valid,

• See if you're able to financially support yourself and your family members in Canada,

• Ask you a few questions to make sure you still meet the terms to immigrate to Canada,

• Confirm your Canadian mailing address, so they can mail your permanent resident card (PR card).

If you change your address within 180 days of completing your interview, you must tell them.

If you're currently working in Canada…

You may be eligible for a bridging open work permit (BOWP - https://www.canada.ca/en/immigration-refugees-citizenship/services/work-canada/extend-permit/bridging-open-work-permit.html) if you are approved in principle for permanent residence. If you're eligible, this permit can let you keep working while you wait for a final decision on your permanent residence application.

You can apply for a BOWP with your permanent residence application but we won't process your BOWP application until you're approved in principle for permanent residence.

If you're outside Canada…

When you arrive in Canada, you'll be greeted by a border services officer (BSO): https://www.canada.ca/en/services/immigration-citizenship/helpcentre/glossary.html#border_services_officer.

When you arrive, you must have:

• A valid passport and/or travel documents. Your passport must be a regular, private passport. You can't immigrate to Canada with a diplomatic, government service or public affairs passport.

• A valid permanent resident visa and your COPR. The BSO will make sure you're entering Canada before or on the expiry date shown on your visa (this document cannot be extended).

The BSO will:

• Make sure all your documents are valid,

• See if you're able to financially support yourself and your family members in Canada,

• Ask you a few questions to make sure you still meet the eligibility requirements to immigrate to Canada,

• Confirm your Canadian mailing address, so we can mail your permanent resident card (PR card).

You won't be allowed into Canada if you:

• Give false or incomplete information or

• Don't convince the officer that you meet the conditions to enter Canada.

If you meet the requirements, the BSO will allow you to enter Canada as a permanent resident. They will also confirm your Canadian mailing address and have your permanent resident card mailed to you there.

If you change your address or contact information within 180 days of arriving in Canada, you must tell them.

If your permanent residence application is refused…

If your application is refused, they'll send you a letter that tells you why.

13.4. How to Find a Job as a Nanny from your Home Country Step by Step

When applying for a job, pay extra attention to the instructions given by the potential employer (agencies or families). Some will demand that you have a certification in first aid and CPR.

1. Signup to Top Job Listings Websites in Canada and Apply

Tweak your resume to be in accord with the job advert. Do not make the mistake many people make of sending one CV to all job postings. Recruiters do not have the time to review all CV's so they adopt a computer shortlisting technology that searches for keywords they are interested in; some of these keywords can mostly be found in the job posting.

When you identify the right keywords, ensure it appears two, three, or four times in your resume. You can also search the organization on LinkedIn, go to job listings, and apply there. You can also connect with the HR or recruiter.

https://canadiannanny.ca/.

https://www.preferrednannies.com/.

https://www.nannyservices.ca/default.asp.

https://www.internationalnannies.com/online-nanny-application.

https://spectrumhealthcare.com/jobs.

https://seniorsforseniors.ca/employment.

https://www.paramed.com/careers/#talcura-careers.

https://victoriannannies.ca/nannies-caregiver-employment-canada/.

https://trafalgarpersonnel.com/overseas-lcp-applicants.

http://www.diamondpersonnel.com/for-caregivers/overseas-applicants/.

https://www.nursenextdoor.com/job-application-form/.

https://www.saskjobs.ca/jsp/jobsearch/advanced.jsp.

http://www.workvantage.ca.

https://www.homecareontario.ca/our-members/list-of-members.

https://bccare.ca/jobs/.

2. Apply to Home Care/Support Worker Recruiting Agencies or Headhunters.

Recruiting agencies are tasked with the responsibility of finding the right candidates for this kind of job; unfortunately, most time they don't get to fill in these vacancies mostly because there are more vacancies than applicants.

Make the recruiting agencies' job easy by applying – they have been looking for you. Below is a list of recruiting agencies/headhunters. You can search for more on google by typing in the right keywords such as "home support worker recruiting agency in Canada", "home support worker recruiting agency in Nunavut" etc. Send them an e-mail with your cover letter and resume.

a) http://islandrecruiting.com/submit-a-resume/.
53 Grafton Street, Charlottetown, PE
Local Phone Number: (902) 367-3797
Tel: (844) 367-3797
hire@islandrecruiting.com

b) https://globalhire.ca/workers/foreign-workers/foreign-workers-form/.
Toronto: 1-416-708-9885
info@globalhire.ca

c) EO HomeCare
5 Clarence Square Toronto, Ontario M5V 1H1
Tel: 416-256-7776
info@eohomecare.ca

d) Suite 1, 2nd floor, 4529A Hastings St. Burnaby, B.C. V5C 2K3, Canada
Tel: (604) 298-6633
Fax: (604) 298-6655
http://paragon-personnel.com.
https://paragon-personnel.com/Nannies_Application_Form.pdf.
info@paragon-personnel.com

e) http://www.phsa.ca/careers/working-here/contact-us.
Provincial Health Services Authority
PHSA Talent Acquisition
#260 – 1770 West 7th Avenue Vancouver, BC V6J 4Y6 Canada
careers@phsa.ca

f) https://allpersonnel.ca/job-opportunities-available/.
2 County Court Blvd, Suite 400, Brampton, ON L6W 3X7 US/Canada
Toll Free: 1-800-895-8897
info@AllPersonnel.ca or resumes@AllPersonnel.ca

g) 207 Glen Park Road
Ottawa, ON K1B 5B8 Canada 613-219-5712
https://www.ayahnannies.com/contact/.

3. Apply to Home Care/Support Worker Employers directly via their websites

Some employers use the service of job posting websites, some use recruiting agencies while others post these vacancies directly on their websites. Certainly, some use a combination of two or the three options.

How about getting your water directly from the aquifer instead of the stream? If you consider that wise, go to these employers directly via their website and apply.

https://eldercare.com/.

14. How to Crack & Dominate the Canada Job Market

In this chapter you'll learn how to get your desired job inside and outside Canada within a short time of your arrival.

14.1. Types of Employment in Canada

In Canada, you're free to work on the kind of gig that best suits or goes well with you. The followings are the type of employment you can opt in for when you get to Canada.

1. **Full-time Employment** -A permanent or full-time job is the way of working we tend to be most familiar with. In Canada, it generally means working 30 hours or more per week for a single employer and fulfilling your contractual duties.

• **Fixed term** - This is contract like employment which a certain period of time is specify for work. Probably maybe someone has gone for maternity leave, you're going to fill the gap till the person resumes.

• **Permanent employment** - In this type of arrangement, you'll often be entitled to a base salary, regular pay period, vacation time and pay, and all other statutory benefits.

2. **Part-Time employment** - This can range from 20 - 25 hours in a week. Part-time workers sometimes have the option of picking up additional shifts to cover for coworkers who call in sick, or for working extra hours during a particularly busy time of the year.

3. **Contract Employment** - If you thrive on trying different things and working in new environments, contract employment might be for you. Contract employment is work that has a predetermined end date, such as the completion of a specific project or a fixed-term. This type of temporary work includes casual, seasonal, freelance, short-term, or any work with a fixed end date.

4. **Casual employment** - In this kind of employment, you are being called upon anytime for a shift gig. And you're going to be paid handsomely for the job you did.

5. **Apprentice or trainee**: You'll be working under an organization to gain work experience and get paid for the service you render. You're being paid according to your award or registered agreement.

6. **Voluntary Work** - Volunteering is a great way to rack up experience, especially if you're new to Canada, a recent graduate, or switching careers. If you have the financial resources and can dedicate a few hours a week to volunteer with a not-for-profit organization in Canada, it will show your future employer not only your ability to be proactive but your ability to show concern for the well-being of others.

14.2. Job Recruitment Cycle in Canada

Here is what recruitment cycle in Canada looks like:

1. Career Opportunity and Application

Identify the role that best suits your qualifications and career aspirations, and send in your resume and cover letter online. Create a folder for the company and put in your resume used to apply for the job, job advertisement and company description. After that, you wait for the company's response.

Take note of your resume because the recruiter will use applicant tracking system to vet the applications for the ones with the advertised keywords. You need to use the keywords of the job you're applying for i.e., the one they used on the job description. Once the resume is good for hiring, they will notify you for a phone interview. If the application fails, you will be notified through your email for the rejection.

2. Initial Telephone Interview

If your profile matches what the company is looking for, a member of their recruitment team will reach out to you. If possible, an initial telephone interview will be arranged to find out more about you. The speaker will be looking for your communication skills, why you want to work with them, soft skills, hard skills, what you're earning, and what you want to earn etc.

Tip: Speak slowly so that they can hear you clearly.

There are two main things that can affect your phone interview: First is your communication skills and, the second is your salary. Know the price range the companies are paying for the very role you are applying. Do a thorough research about how much they're willing to pay. You can research that by searching the company on www.ziprecruiter.com/?country=ca or www.glassdoor.ca/index.htm.

3. Panel Interviews

If you are considered a potential candidate for the position, you will be invited to attend face-to-face interviews. Conducted by a panel, including the hiring manager, you'll be sitting across from three or more hiring managers and meeting with them all at once in a 45 to 60 minutes interview. They will use this interview to determine your career interests, educational background, skills, competencies, and experience, as well as what motivates you to succeed at work.

Quick Tip Here:

1. Research and remember your interviewers.

2. Bring enough materials for the entire panel.

3. Do not address only the most senior person in the room but engage with every interviewer equally.

4. Do not forget interviewers' names & roles because they want to know your how easily you can remember things.

5. Do not ignore your body language.

6. Be prepared for follow-up questions.

7. Do not get defensive.

8. Ask questions of your own.

4. Assessments

A company may invite you to participate in a psychometric assessment which makes them to better understand your motivation and how you behave at work.

5. Second-Round Interviews

If you successfully complete the panel interview, you will then be invited to participate in a second interview. These interviews will enable both you and the company to assess the potential for future collaboration and for you to get an additional insight into what working with the company is like.

6. Reference Check

They will ask your referees to answer questions about your previous work performance, your skills and behavior at work.

7. Selection Decision and Offer

Company's selection panel will identify the most qualified candidate for the post. Once you have been selected for the role, your HR representative will send you an employment offer and answer any questions you may have.

14.3. Things You Could Be Asked in A Canada Job Interview

1. Why do you think your skills and experience make you a good candidate for this position?

2. What are your strengths and weaknesses?

3. Give me an example of a work situation in which you're proud of your performance. What're some of the factors that contributed to your performance?

4. Tell me about a time you had a conflict at work with a coworker or a customer. How did you handle it?

5. Describe how you would prioritize tasks or needs on the job.

6. You've been asked to take on a new task, one that you've never done before. You want to make sure that you do it well because it could lead to a raise in the future. What're the first steps that you would take?

7. How do you handle stressful situations?

8. Which do you like better, lions or tigers?

9. Tell me about a time when you had to make a difficult decision. What steps did you take and what was the outcome?

10. Tell me about a time when you had to deal with multiple deadlines. How did you handle it?

11. Why should we hire you?

12. Tell me about your experience in this type of workplace.

13. You have an angry customer who has interrupted your conversation with another customer. What will you do?

14. Tell me about a time you had a conflict at work with a co-worker or a customer. How did you handle it?

15. You've been asked to lead a project that involves supervising several co-workers who are also your friends. How would you handle this situation and preserve your relationships?

16. What would you do if you caught one of your co-workers stealing?

17. Tell me about a time you had a conflict at work with a co-worker or a customer. How did you handle it?

18. How are you feeling about your performance in this interview so far?

19. Which do you like better, chocolate, or vanilla ice cream?

14.4. How to Write an Irresistible Canada Standard Resume

If you've received your PPR or probably you've received your ITA, the best thing to do next is start applying for job.

You need to get to the job market when you're right in the process so you won't go flat broke or start going to places with your resume when you arrive Canada. Taking your savings there for spending won't last any longer without any source of income.

Firstly, what you need to do is prepare your resume (CV) to Canada standard. You need to tailor it pretty well to match the interest of the employers and recruiters. I tell you, an average recruiter needs 6 seconds to scan through your resume to know maybe you're a perfect fit or not.

14.4.1. Choosing the Right Format

Resume is something you as a job seeker presents to an employer in order to sell your idea. If what you are presenting is not convincing enough, you won't be considered for interview. Since resume is the marketing tool you're using to market yourself, you need to choose the type of resume that perfectly match what you're applying for.

Here's what your resume should look like. Generally, there are three main types of resume formats you can choose from:

• Chronological Resume

This kind of resume is for you if you have consistent professional experience, no large employment gaps, and intend to continue working in the same field you've been working before. This format is widely used and preferred by many recruiters and job sites. Figure 14.4.1 and Figure 14.4.2 show samples of this kind of resume.

CHRONOLOGICAL RESUME
TEACHER EDUCATION STUDENT

Chris Anderson-Reed
1234 - 4th Avenue
San Francisco, CA 94118
415-555-1212
careed@usfca.edu
www.linkedin.com/chrisandersonreed

OBJECTIVE

Elementary School Classroom Teacher: Prefer grades K-4, willing to teach other levels

EDUCATION

M.A., Teaching, University of San Francisco, CA   05/13
SB 2042 Multiple Subject Credential with English Learner Authorization

B.A. History, Mills College, Oakland, CA   05/10

TEACHING EXPERIENCE

Student Teacher, Fourth Grade
BALBOA ELEMENTARY, San Francisco, CA   10/12 – 12/12
  • Teach math, reading, English and social studies in a class of thirty-one multicultural students, including seven students with special learning needs.
  • Design units in children's literature incorporating multi-ethnic themes.
  • Develop lessons in critical thinking skills using math games.

Student Teacher, Kindergarten
GARDEN GROVE ELEMENTARY, San Francisco, CA   01/12 – 03/12
  •Taught math and whole language instruction to a class of thirty-five multicultural students.
  •Developed and presented lesson unit on Chinese New Year which included construction of Chinese Dragon and presentation to two other classes.
  •Prepared and presented an African History unit in celebration of Black History Month.

Instructional Assistant, First Grade
VISTA ELEMENTARY, South San Francisco, CA   09/11 – 12/11
  •Directed groups in various developmental and educational activities.

OTHER WORK EXPERIENCE

Office Manager
OFFICE SERVICES, INC., San Francisco, CA   07/10 - 08/11
  •Managed administrative functions for 25 person consulting firm.

ADDITIONAL SKILLS

Conversational Spanish
Play piano and guitar

Figure 14.4.1: First sample of a chronological resume

147

PHIL PATTERSON

(555) 555-5555 ● example@example.com ● Richmond, VA

PROFESSIONAL SUMMARY

Devoted to giving every patient high-quality and cost-effective support to reduce complaints and address root causes. Effective in emergencies in addition to routine needs such as chart updating and patient and family education. Well-versed in the latest medical studies and treatments.

WORK HISTORY

Nov 2015 - Current
Richmond, VA

Urgent Care Physician / Richmond Urgent Care
● Consulted with up to 20 patients each day to review physical conditions and make care plans.
● Provided expert critical care response in emergency situations involving illnesses or injuries.
● Effectively reduced symptoms and treated underlying conditions by prescribing targeted medications and therapies.

Aug 2012 - Oct 2015
Richmond, VA

Doctor / Patient First
● Evaluated patient histories, complaints and current symptoms to understand conditions and begin diagnostic processes.
● Implemented therapeutic regiments involving medications and other interventions to mitigate symptoms and prevent reoccurrence.
● Conferred with specialists to obtain expertise on patient conditions and referred individuals in need of additional care.

May 2009 - May 2012
Charlottesville, VA

Resident Physician / University Hospital
● Shadowed attending physicians during complex and innovative procedures to gain greater understanding of technique.
● Interviewed patients concerning physical complaints, discussed symptoms, asked questions and suggested treatment options.
● Stayed abreast of advances in treatments, emerging pharmaceutical applications and new diagnostic tools for application in adult medicine.

SKILLS

● Urgent care
● Patient examination
● Diagnosing conditions
● Preventive care expert

● Medical records management
● Prescribing medications
● Patient treatment planning

EDUCATION

2009
Charlottesville, VA

M.D.
University of Virginia

2005
Williamsburg, VA

Bachelor of Science in Pre-Medicine
College of William And Mary

Figure 14.4.2: Second sample of a chronological resume

• Functional Resume

This resume is for you if you've changed, have several gaps or switched career path.

148

Adam Patrick Jones
7315 West Oyster Street, Brewerton, NY 13503
Home: (315) 656-3212 • Cell: (315) 228-6654 • Email: adampjones@gmail.com

---

EDUCATION

Associate in Science, Business Administration   **May 2012**
Onondaga Community College, Syracuse, New York
GPA 3.46

HIGHLIGHTS OF QUALIFICATIONS

- Served 8 years in the U.S. Military with 7 years experience in office administration.
- Supervisory experience including 5 years of supervising a group of 10 staff members.
- Skilled in purchasing, inventory management, budgeting, bookkeeping, customer service
- Proficient with Microsoft Word and Microsoft Excel, and Microsoft Access.
- Experience with a variety of office equipment including: scanners, photocopiers, printers, and fax machines
- Languages: English, French and Spanish

ACCOMPLISHMENTS

Leadership
- Successfully lead the 5 person Administrative Services team to keep the schedules of senior executives and ensure full attendance at scheduled meetings.
- Supervised over 10 personnel whose duties included filing office forms and stocking office equipment.
- Managed the distribution of office supplies including office desks, filing cabinets and office chairs valued at over $200K.

Administration
- Performed record keeping and document handling, bookkeeping and budgeting for the Office of the Deputy Chief of Staff for Personnel.
- Saved 6 man-hours per month on the Receiving Office Supplies process by changing the sequence of steps.
- Purchased office supplies including printers, ink cartridges and copy paper for the Office of the Deputy Chief of Staff for Personnel.
- Received and distributed relocation orders for enlisted personnel.

Training
- Delivered highly effective time management training monthly over a period of 5 years as an on-the-job trainer.
- Trained 7 Administrative Clerks in completing and maintaining accurate duty schedules .
- Provided exceptional administrative training twice a month over a period of 2 years as an on-the-job trainer.

WORK HISTORY

Administrative Supervisor
2005 - 2007   *U.S. Army, Fort Bragg, N. Carolina*

Administrative Assistant
2002 - 2005   *U.S. Army, US Army 32d Air Defense Command, Germany*

Administrative Clerk
1999 - 2002   *U.S. Army, Fort Meade, Maryland*

PROFESSIONAL TRAINING

2004   **Time Management** - *U.S. Army*
2003   **Purchasing** - *U.S. Army*
2002   **Personnel Management** - *Prime Management Consultants*

Figure 14.4.3: First sample of a functional resume

149

LINDA MOWRY
348 Somerset Road; Hayward, CA 94541
(510) 123-4567 or Linda.Mowry@email.com

OBJECTIVE: A position as Sales Coordinator, Representative or Account Executive.

SUMMARY OF QUALIFICATIONS
- Twelve years successful experience in direct sales of a range of products and services.
- Extensive practical hands-on experience as co-owner & manager of a small business.
- Motivated and enthusiastic about developing good relations with clients.
- Professional in appearance and presentation.

RELEVANT SKILLS
SALES & NEW ACCOUNT DEVELOPMENT
Increased a small publication's advertising revenue through market research and promotion.
Developed new distribution outlets for a special-interest magazine in Northern California
- Made cold calls and follow-up visits to retail outlets throughout the region.
- Organized detailed routebooks and financial recordkeeping.
- Successfully increased readership by more than 40 percent over a two-year period.
CUSTOMER RELATIONS
Served as vendor representative for Jana Imports:
- Coordinated product information and distribution for 75 field representatives and major accounts.
- Promoted giftware products at trade shows throughout the region.
- Handled face-to-face contacts with new and established customers.
Oversaw the production of advertising and its placement in major trade publications.
ADVERTISING, MARKETING, DISTRIBUTION
Organized and styled merchandise for effective presentation in a 20-page giftware catalog.
Kept accurate, current computer records of inventory, international suppliers, brokers, shippers, etc.
Handled all aspects of order taking and processing, both at Bill's Dairy and Jana Imports.

EMPLOYMENT HISTORY

2004-present	Sales Coordinator	Jana Imports, Oakland, CA
1998-2003	Distribution Coordinator	Déjà vu Publishing, San Rafael, CA
1993-1998	Co-owner/Manager	Bill's Dairy, Livermore, OR

EDUCATION
Bay City College, San Francisco, BA in Liberal Arts

Figure 14.4.4: Second sample of a functional resume

• Combination

This kind of resume is for you if you have several or diverse background of experience. This is most used when skills and abilities are required but not experience. This one is for job seekers who want to show off their skills and qualifications.

Combination Resume Format for Canada

Name and Contact information

Summary/Objective

Skills and Abilities

Professional Experience

Figure 14.4.5: First sample of a combination resume

NATHAN AYERS

895 12TH ST., CARMINE, TX 78932 (555) 555-5555 EXAMPLE@EXAMPLE.COM

PROFESSIONAL SUMMARY

Professional sales-focused Assistant manager with years of management experience in diverse fields. Proven history of building relationships with satisfied customers. Equally skilled as management leader and meticulous number cruncher focused on overall operational performance.

RELEVANT SKILLS

- Skilled in training employees and leveraging organized approaches to handle daily planning, scheduling and customer service requirements.
- Excellent reputation for resolving problems, improving customer satisfaction, and driving overall operational improvements.
- Consistently saved costs while increasing profits.

SKILLS

- Team management
- Conflict resolution
- Operational improvement
- Customer Service
- Extremely organized
- Strong verbal communication
- Team leadership
- Trend assessment

WORK HISTORY

MARCH 2018-CURRENT

Assistant Manager | Durby Crossing | Waco, TX

- Boosted sales rates 25% by checking for and locating requested items in inventory system.
- Supported staff development and goal attainment by focusing on skill development and job satisfaction.
- Monitored employee performance and developed improvement plans.

FEBRUARY 2014-JUNE 2016

Retail Assistant Manager | Forever 21 | Bendena, TX

- Returned change and currency and processed debit and credit card payments with 100% accuracy rate.
- Liaised with retail manager to cultivate and maintain positive and uplifting work environment and family-centric culture.
- Managed expenses and developed strategies that positioned store to perform in accordance with budget.

MARCH 2011-NOVEMBER 2013

Sales Associate | Old Navy | Langley, TX

- Kept on top of changes to store products and promotions to maintain strong sales.
- Supported loss prevention goals by maintaining accurate drawers and monitoring shopper behavior.
- Offered each customer top-notch, personal service and polite support to boost sales and customer satisfaction.

EDUCATION

Some College (No Degree):
Texas A&M University, College Station, TX

Figure 14.4.6: Second sample of a combination resume

14.4.2. Tailor Your Resume to Each Application

Every item on your resume should be written with your target job in mind. Carefully examine on how the information you want to add matches the job you're applying for; if it doesn't match, then it shouldn't be added to it. Again, research is essential. The more you know about a prospective employer, the better you can convey how you would be an asset to them. Be crisp, detailed, yet straight to the point, don't get carried away with adding unimportant information.

14.4.3. Keep it Short & Sweet

A career summary must be briefly discussed; describe the skills and experiences which most appropriate with the job which you're applying. It should be specific to you - if it's vague enough that it could apply to anyone in your field, it doesn't provide any benefit. If you're new to a field, or even just new to the workforce, then a career summary is not necessary.

For your work history, it must have action words like: applied, trained, maintained, organized, implemented. All must be in the past tense to show that they're in the past even if you're still working there.

14.4.4. Write the Important Qualifications

You need to mention at least "three" of the specified qualities in the job description, also explain how you have demonstrated these qualities. Don't be modest or undercut yourself. If you are unsure on how to do it, discuss your experience with colleagues, or friends or relatives. They probably might give you some perspective on what you've achieved. Now match up the two sections on 'responsibilities' and 'achievements' and write about them on your resume.

14.4.5. Industry Specific Resume

Your resume is the most financially important document you will ever own. Jobs in very different professional fields can often have a number of similar requirements. So, what are the skills you've already demonstrated that are applicable? They may be more than you think.

Consider these possibilities:

- Time management

- Project management

- Collaboration

- Persuasive communication

You should also be prepared to speak about what motivates you to choose a career change. You can add a little of this into your objective, then also be prepared to give a brief of it in your cover letter, and then of course speak to it when you land an interview.

14.4.6. Add Volunteer Experience

Volunteer means working or performing service for free and without mind or receiving payback later. Working as volunteer can help you gain Canadian work experience. There must be a section in your resume that must have Volunteer Experience because most of these companies are big on Corporate Social Responsibility (CSR).

They want to see that you have the heart of giving back and that, you've done that before. Even companies oftentimes (maybe a few days before paying salaries) give workers time to go and volunteer somewhere.

14.5. How to Get a Job in Canada If You're Outside Canada

Create a LinkedIn profile

The first thing I'll tell you is to create a LinkedIn account if you have none. To do that, go to https://linkedin.com. Once you're logged in, fill all the details on your LinkedIn profile to stay relevant and unique. You can search for one or two Youtube videos to learn how to create a professional Linkedin profile.

Here are the things you need to update on your profile to attract recruiters and employers:

Upload a professional headshot

Look relaxed and attractive and make sure to put on a smile. Dress really smart. Whether you choose to wear a full suit or simply a smart shirt is yours to decide, but no employer will dismiss you for dressing smartly. Don't use a cropped picture of groups as your profile picture or picture with a distracting background.

Add description of your professional accomplishments

Filling out your professional description is much like writing a CV, it is rarely good enough to add the company names and the dates of employment. When writing this section, you should include both information about the positions you've held and "your accomplishments in these positions if they're relevant to the types of roles you're applying for.

Add a friendly, to-the-point Summary

Your summary has an important position on your profile so it's much needed to get it right. Your summary should contain your experience, your strengths, your skills, and your vision for your career.

Also Add the following...

- four, five, or more skills, even better if they're endorsed!

- You must add detailed descriptions of your education

- Add a compelling headline.

- Add many Linkedin connections

To earn the all-important All-Star status on LinkedIn, you'll need to have at least 100 connections. So, make connections with Canadian people, not friends from your country. An example is shown in Figure 14.5.1.

Figure 14.5.1: A sample professional Linkedin profile

Format your resume to a Canadian style

I have explained that earlier. Now, the next thing here is get your proposal and CV ready because offers will be coming your way and you'll need them to apply for the gig.

Start searching for jobs and apply

The best way to get a job is to check with your acquaintances if they have an open position in their team. But most of the new immigrants barely have any connections in Canada. So, do the job search the normal way on LinkedIn, www.ca.indeed.com/ and other websites you may know.

14.6. Six Proven Steps to Secure a Job Within 30 Days of Arriving in Canada

1. Put Together a Killer Resume

Your resume is what represents you during your job hunt. It's important to make sure it reflects everything you have to offer. Even though you don't have a long work history to include, you have your education and key skills that you want to share with potential employers.

For instance, are you an extrovert who's great at working with people? Are you the one your friends turn to for help getting organized? Do you know how to use Photoshop reasonably well? Let employers know about these skills! If you're not sure how to start, check out more resume writing tips on Google.

2. Tap into The Hidden Markets

Did you know that as many as half of all job opportunities are not publicly advertised? So, how do all these unposted job opportunities find applicants? Often, they're filled internally or by friends and family members of current employees.

Sometimes even recruiters don't bother posting niche jobs online if they know they'll be flooded with unqualified applicants. After all, what's the point in receiving an application if it's not worth the time it takes to read? To tap into this market of unposted jobs, ask friends and family if they know of opportunities at their workplace.

3. Consider Internships

Summer jobs don't have to be limited to job titles like 'camp counselor' and 'burger flipper.' If you're looking for a simple no-stress way to make some cash for the summer, these jobs are perfect. However, if you're in school and looking for ways to expand on your education, an internship or co-op position may be a great idea. There are both paid and unpaid opportunities available, so keep an eye out for ones that fit you.

4. Act Decently on Social Media Face

In today's smartphone-driven culture, everyone and their mom have a social media presence. Don't make the mistake of thinking that hiring managers aren't looking at your profiles and judging what kind of employee you might be, based on how you act on social media.

You might think those silly drunk photos you posted last summer are funny, but a hiring manager probably won't see things the same way. Before applying for a summer job, give your social media accounts a quick sweep and delete anything that you see to be inappropriate or hinder your chances of landing a killer summer job.

5. Don't Be Random. Rather Focus on a Few Applications

The internet space is flooded with job opportunities, so it can be tempting to slap together a generic resume and submit it to as many jobs as you can, then wait and see who takes you up. That's the wrong way to look at applying for a job, even a summer job.

Hiring managers are looking for passionate people who stand out from a crowd. If you're submitting the same application to every job under the sun, it's a guarantee that won't be the case. Take a little more time refining application for jobs you really want. If you're being tempted to apply for a job you don't really want, don't!

6. Think Beyond City Centers

If you're a city dweller, it's easy to forget that there's a place beyond the urban jungle you live in. Job seekers often write off jobs that are out of the city limits. Small towns and suburbs need jobs filled too, and chances are the competition for these jobs is going to be a lot lower than those in densely populated urban areas.

14.7. Other Helpful Resources

Want to check how your resume matches up against the job description?

1. Check www.jobscan.co. Copy and paste the job description side by side with your uploaded resume to see what score you get. Treat your job search like a marketing project.

2. Use a job search organizing and networking strategy app like jibberjobber (www.jibberjobber.com/login.php) to help you stay focused and on track with your project plan.

Do you want to meet a Canadian expert in your industry over Skype/Zoom or a cup of coffee? Use LinkedIn to target companies and the people who work in the role you're seeking, and build relationships with them first before asking for favors!

Now if you thoroughly go through all the tips I've compiled above, you have nothing to stop you in securing a job that suits your career path.

14.8. Portals to Get Notified of Job Openings

1. Askmigration.com.

Visit https://askmigration.com/a-canadian-mp-wants-approved-pr-applicants-to-be-allowed-to-enter-the-country/.

Fill in your name, job role and email address that you want to be receiving job alert on. Then click on the subscribe button and you're good to go.

2. Jobboom.com.

Visit https://www.jobboom.com/en/job/.

Type in your job role and city, then hit search button.

Input your email then hit "create alert" button.

3. Google Careers.

Visit https://careers.google.com/jobs/results/.

Search Google Careers with any criteria you like.

Scroll to the middle of the page and click "Turn on job alerts for your search"

Under Frequency, set how often you'd like to get the alert (daily, weekly, or monthly).

Click Save, and watch your inbox regularly.

You'll only receive emails from Google Careers if new jobs that match your search criteria have been posted.

4. Indeed.

Visit https://ca.indeed.com/Foreign-Worker-Canada-jobs.

Enter your email into the email address on the page and hit "send me new jobs"

There will be a pop-up to verify through your email.

5. Subscribe to Jooble.

Visit https://ca.jooble.org/jobs-canada-hiring-foreign-workers.

Type in you're the job role you want and specify the location then hit "find job" button.

Click on "Get new jobs by email" button.

There will be a pop-up window. Put in your email and hit subscribe button.

Type in your Canada city or you may prefer to skip it.

Go to your email inbox, locate the message from Jooble, open it and verify your account.

Now, you'll be receiving job alert from Jooble.

14.9. Top Recruiting Agencies that Target International Applicants

An international recruitment agency specializes in helping firms find the right global candidates for their human resources needs. Should you use a job agent?

1. Job agents do it right for you to get your job because they know they have their cut in that.

2. When a recruiter gets the job for you, that means he will take his own share, maybe before or after, and you don't need looking around for a job again. The job is already there for you because they know where to go and not to go. They've been around for a very long time.

3. Job agents interview you themselves and tell you things to add and remove from your resume because in the long run it will actually be a plus for you.

14.9.1. Top 40 Canadian Recruiters & Contacts

1. Quebec International: http://www.quebecinternational.ca/.
Address: 1035, Wilfrid-Pelletier, Suite 400, Québec City (Québec) G1W 0C5
Phone No.: 1 418 681-9700

2. Hays Recruitment Canada: https://www.hays.ca/.
Address: Calgary, AB T2P 0S4, Canada
Phone No.: +1 403-269-4297

3. Global Hire: https://globalhire.ca.
Address: Global Hire Placement Services Edmonton, AB T6B 3S3, Canada
Phone No.: +1 780-439-3651

4. Petro Staff International: http://www.petro-staff.com/.
Address: Suite 280, 23 Sunpark Drive S.E. Calgary, Alberta, Canada T2X 3V1

Phone No.: (403) 266-8988

5. Cowan International: http://www.cowaninternational.com/.
Address: 222 Main Road, Hudson, Quebec Canada. J0P 1H0
Phone No.: +1.450.458.0101

6. Drake International: https://ca.drakeintl.com/.
Address: 13222 118 Avenue, Edmonton, Alberta T5L 4N4
Phone No.: 780 414 6341

7. Diamond Personnel: http://www.diamondpersonnel.com/.
Address: 1000 Sheppard Ave W, North York, ON M3H 2T6, Canada
Toronto: 416-730-8866
Vancouver: 604-484-4966
Calgary: 403-351-0179

8. Michael Page: http://www.michaelpage.ca/.
Address: 130 Adelaide Street West. Suite 1900. Toronto, ON M5H 3P5.
Canada.
Phone No.: +1 416 306 3900.
9. Outpost Recruitment - http://outpostrecruitment.com/.
Address: Vancouver, BC.
Phone No.: 778-861-1244

10. Alliance Online
Address: 201 Portage Ave 18th Floor, Winnipeg, MB R3B 3K6, Canada
Phone No.: +1204-583-6387

11. Island Recruiting; http://www.allianceonline.ca/.
Address: Charlottetown, PE C1A 1K8, Canada
Phone No.: +1 902-367-3797

12. ELI: http://www.eurolabour.ca/wp/.
Address: Euro Labour Infusion Ltd. 17 – 1700 Varsity Estates Drive NW
Calgary, Alberta T3B 2W9, Canada
Phone No.: (403) 262-7141

13. Work Global Canada : https://www.workglobalcanada.com/recruitment-services/international-programs/.
Address: St. John's, NL A1A 1W8, Canada
Phone No.: +1 709-700-1983

14. IIERC :http://www.iierc.com/.
Address: Suite 102, 5677 – 99 Street, Edmonton, AB T6E 3N8
Fax: 780-669-3946

15. Canada Connect: http://canadaconnectimmigration.ca/.
Address: 169 Marion Street, Winnipeg, Manitoba. R2H 0T3, Located on Main Floor
Phone No.: 204-221-1199, Toll-Free: 1-855-454-9129

16. Robert L. Holmes Professional Placement – Employment Agency and Recruiter in Cambridge Ontario
Address: Cambridge Ontario, Canada
Phone No.: +1 519-621-4373

17. Fuze HR solutions Inc – Brampton
Address: Brampton, ON, Canada
Phone No.: +1 905-361-3987

18. Liberty Staffing Services Inc.
Address: Stratford, ON, Canada
Phone No.: +1 519-275-2742

19. Brockwell Services Recruitment Agency
Address: Pickering, ON, Canada
Phone No.: +1 416-306-9998

20. Adecco Durham Region, Employment agency in Oshawa
Address: Employment agency in Oshawa, Canada
Phone No.: +1 905-436-6202

21. Recruiting in Motion – Oakville/Burlington
Address: Burlington, ON, Canada
Phone No.: +1 905-863-6428

22. Milton Employment Partners Centre
Address: Milton, ON, Canada
Phone No.: +1 905-693-8458

23. First Choice Employment – Best Recruitment Agency in Toronto
Address: Employment agency in Toronto, Canada
Phone No.: +1 416-247-0001

24. David Aplin Group
Address: Mississauga, ON, Canada
Phone No.: +1 905-566-9700

25. York Employment Services Inc.
Address: Ontario, CA, United States
Phone No.: +1 909-581-0181

26. Durham Recruiting
Address: Oshawa, ON, Canada
Phone No.: +1 905-579-2950

27. Hunt Personnel Employment Agency
Address: Toronto, ON, Canada
Phone No.: +1 416-492-8500

28. Summit Search Group
Address: Oakville, ON, Canada
Phone No.: +1 905-257-9300

29. Randstad Canada
Address: Mississauga, ON, Canada
Phone No.: +1 905-814-6554

30. Canadian Staffing Consultants Ltd.
Address: Markham, ON, Canada
Phone No.: +1 905-604-5545

31. Canadian International Recruitment Services Inc
Address: Toronto, ON M5C 2B6, Canada
Phone No.: +60 11-2180 9461
32. Goldbeck Recruiting
Address: Vancouver, BC V6B 4M9, Canada
Phone No.: +1 604-684-1428

33. International Labor Centre & Immigration Recruitment Services Canada Inc
Address: Saskatoon, SK S7N 2G8, Canada
Phone No.: +1 306-242-4024

34. Renard International Hospitality Search Consultants
Address: Toronto, ON M5H 2K1, Canada
Phone No.: +1 416-364-8325

35. QForce Canada, Employment Job Placement Agency
Address: Whitby, ON L1N 3K5, Canada
Phone No.: +1 844-243-2225

36. Angus One Professional Recruitment Ltd
Address: Vancouver, BC V6Z 1S4, Canada
Phone No.: +1 604-682-8367

38. TEKsystems
Address: Burnaby, BC V5G 4X7, Canada
Phone No.: +1 604-412-3500

39. WorkVantage
Address: Edmonton, AB T5J 3R8, Canada
Phone No.: +1 403-450-3432

40. Planet4iT Recruitment Agency
Address: Toronto, ON M5E 1J4, Canada
Phone No.: +1 416-363-9888

14.10. Why Many Job Applicants from Outside Canada Don't Get Response

Below are the top reasons an employer don't get back to many job applicants, and how you can take advantage of this.

1. The job was already filled

Sometimes companies merely post job openings, even though they already have an internal candidate in mind for the position. These employers often have company policies that require them to post job openings to the public, but in reality, there isn't any position available.

In addition, some employers don't take down job postings after they've been filled. Why? A lot of times jobs gets posted and then picked up by other job boards, so employers don't always know where their job postings are. So, it's important to apply as soon as you see a job you like.

2. HR was flooded with applications

Simply put, some hiring managers just don't have the time to check every job application they receive. This frequently occurs when an employer receives hundreds of applications for a position but only has one person reviewing them.

3. Applicants didn't follow instructions

Job postings often state what candidates must submit with their application. Applicants should follow these instructions to the letter. For example, maybe the employer required you to submit a cover letter, but you didn't, or the employer asked you to submit your resume as a PDF but you submitted it as a Word document.

Moreover, a lot of employers will use job application instructions as a test to see how closely candidates read directions. So, if an application requires two writing samples and you submit one, guess what? You're not going to be considered for the position. You can't say that you're detail oriented and then fail to follow the instructions in the job posting.

4. Applicants submit their applications the wrong way

First, you'll want to cross check that you've applied for the job very correctly. This seems obvious, but it's an easy mistake to make. For example, you may have e-mailed your resume and other application materials when it clearly states in the job posting that everything should be submitted through their application portal.

Maybe you didn't catch that instruction the first time around but don't fret. If you realize you made a mistake along the way, do what you can to remedy the situation (i.e., reapply and send a brief apology note to the hiring manager explaining what happened.

5. Applicant's salary requirements were too high

Many states have made it illegal for companies to ask job candidates about their salary history, but that ban isn't in place nationwide. Unfortunately, many online systems don't let you skip questions, which means you need to put something down for your current salary.

However, if your number exceeds what the company has allocated for the position, your application may not even reach the hiring manager's desk. The upshot? Some employers say what the salary range is in the posting, so, if you know the job you're interviewing for pays less than what you're making and you're OK with that, state it on your application.

6. Applicants' resumes weren't tailored to the job description

Today, many employers use application tracking systems (ATS) to vet job applications. These software programs screen resumes by searching for certain keywords, which typically appear in the job posting. To pass this initial test, use the job advert as a guide.

If the job posting says the employer is looking for an experienced professional who is "fluent in data analytics," use the phrase "fluent in data analytics" (assuming you're in fact are) on your resume. The ATS will pick up on the phrase and realize it matches up with the job description.

7. Applicants didn't customize their applications to the open position

In today's tough job market, every resume should be crafted in response to the requested experience and responsibilities listed in the job description. You'll want to take the time to tailor your resume, as well as your cover letter and any other application materials, to the job at hand. This not only helps you avoid the resume black hole and make it through the applicant tracking system, but also shows the employer you are truly interested in the job and willing to put in effort to prove it. Not customizing your application makes you appear lazy and that's not the message you're sending.

8. Applicants weren't the right fit

This one tends to be the bitterest pill to swallow. In many cases, you won't hear back from an employer because you simply weren't a good match for the position, or there was someone who was an even better match than you were. It happens. But it doesn't mean you're hopeless by any stretch.

9. Applicants were not qualified

By all accounts, you think that you're more than qualified for the position. But when a potential employer reads your resume and cover letter, they may have a different opinion. For whatever reason it might be (e.g., you don't have the necessary skills, you're missing a particular certification required for the job, your cover letter had grammatical errors, etc.), you're just not the right person for the position. But technically, a company might not legally be able to tell you what's wrong, so the employer likely won't respond to your application.

14.11. All You Need to Secure a Job Offer Within Canada

Whether you are applying in Canada or outside Canada, you will need…

1. A resume to apply.

2. You will need a Social Insurance Number (SIN). A SIN is a 9-digit number you need to work in Canada or to use government programs and get benefits. Your employer uses your SIN on forms that they have to fill out related to your work. For example, your SIN goes on income tax, Employment Insurance, and Canada Pension Plan forms.

14.11.1. How to Apply for SIN Online

To apply online you will need to upload copies of a few different documents. They are as follows:

1. A valid primary document that proves your identity and legal status in Canada.

2. A valid secondary document to confirm your identity.

3. An acceptable proof of address.

If the name indicated on your primary or secondary document is different than the name you are currently using, you must also provide supporting documents.

14.11.2. How to Apply for SIN by Email

To apply by mail you will need:

1. A completed SIN application form (if you are unable to print the application form, you can order the form by phone at 1-506-548-7961; long-distance charges may apply).

2. The required original documents.

You will need to mail your completed application form and original documents (photocopies are not accepted) to the Social Insurance Registration Office. If you send your application by registered mail, your document(s) will be returned to you in the same way. Service Canada is not responsible for documents lost in the mail.

Once you have submitted your application, the legislation does not prevent you from working in insurable employment before you receive your SIN.

14.11.3. How to Apply for SIN in Person

You can request an appointment using the online service request form.

1. Get an application form online or from your local Service Canada Centre.

2. Fill it out.

3. Collect the documents you need.

4. Take your application and documents to your local Service Canada Centre.

If you meet all the requirements, you can get your Social Insurance Number (SIN) the day you hand in the application. Service Canada no longer provides plastic SIN cards. There is no application fee for your first SIN.

5. You'll need a mobile phone number they can reach you on.

How to get a Canadian number

1. Buy yourself a MagicJack and set it up with a Canadian number. This way you'll have 2-way talk, voicemail, and can even use their mobile app on a cell phone.

2. Another way is to sign up for NetTalk Canada. This has a similar idea as MagicJack.

3. Sign up for free Fongo/Freephoneonline service and run it smoothly on any of the devices.

14.12. Additional Job Resources

Browse job search websites and newspapers classified sections to see who is hiring. There are various job portals that have thousands of job postings online for you to choose from. A few examples are:

• Indeed Canada: https://ca.indeed.com/

• Glassdoor: https://www.glassdoor.com/

• Eluta: https://www.eluta.ca/

• Monster: https://www.monster.ca

• JobBank: https://www.jobbank.gc.ca

• Workopolis: https://www.workopolis.com

• SaskJob: https://www.saskjobs.ca/jsp/jobsearch/advanced.jsp

• WorkVantage: http://www.workvantage.ca

• Simply Hired: https://www.simplyhired.ca/

• CareerBuilder: https://www.careerbuilder.ca/

• BcCare: https://bccare.ca/jobs/

• WorkBc: https://www.workbc.ca/jobs-careers/find-jobs/jobs.aspx

14.12.1. More Helpful Resources (Videos included)

1. What You Need to Know to Secure a Job Offer from Outside or Within Canada: https://www.youtube.com/watch?v=QgCHbt7Jhws&t=6388s.

2. How to Win Job Interviews from an Interview Expert and Author: https://www.youtube.com/watch?v=pUx6L1Xf9E0.

3. Some employment agencies:

https://clutch.co/ca/hr/recruiting.

https://www.jobseem.com/top-recruitment-agencies-in-canada-job-consultancy.

14.12.2. How to Get Further Help

Thank you very much for reading my book. I hope you really learn many new things from it. If you need further help in your application for Canada permanent residency, study or work in Canada, don't hesitate to contact me through my support email below. I will get back to you very quickly. If you'd like to share your travel success story with me, send it through my email below.

Cheers,

Ojula Technology Innovations
OjulaTech@gmail.com

Made in the USA
Monee, IL
09 December 2022

20276699R00096